D0443290

Touched by the Anointing

Touched by the Anointing

By
Rod Parsley

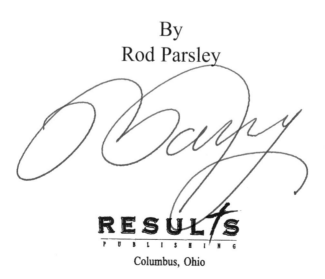

RESULTS
PUBLISHING
Columbus, Ohio

TOUCHED BY THE ANOINTING
Copyright © 2004, by Rod Parsley
All Rights Reserved.
Printed in the United States of America.
ISBN 1-880244-88-8

Published by:

Results Publishing
World Harvest Church
P.O. Box 32932
Columbus, Ohio 43232

This book or parts thereof may not be reproduced
in any form without written permission from the
publisher.

Unless otherwise noted, all Scripture references
are from the King James Version of the Bible.

Scripture taken from THE AMPLIFIED BIBLE.
Old Testament copyright © 1965, 1987 by the
Zondervan Corporation. The Amplified New
Testament copyright © 1958, 1987 by The
Lockman Foundation. Used by permission.

TABLE OF CONTENTS

YOUR TIME HAS COME

We are living in the day of the supernatural. Everywhere you look, God is moving with a mighty hand upon His people.

From the time of Elijah to the days Jesus walked the streets of Jerusalem to the miracles performed through Peter and Paul, there has been a power available to set the most helpless captive free. That power is called the anointing of God.

The anointing was in Moses's face, shining when he came down out of the mountain. It was in Moses's rod that broke up the Red Sea. The anointing was present in Elijah's mantle as he smote the Jordan River and the waters parted.

The power of the anointing is still at work today in the lives of Christians around the world. Its power is available to arrest the most debilitating and life-threatening disease. Most of all, this power can transport a life from the clutches of hell to the glory of heaven.

The power of the anointing is available to every believer. The Bible says of Jesus,

> And he said unto them, Go ye into all the world, and preach the gospel to every crea-ture. He that believeth and is baptized shall be saved; but he that believeth not shall be damned. And these signs shall follow them that believe; In my name shall they cast out devils; they shall speak with new tongues; They shall take up serpents; and if they drink any deadly thing, it shall not hurt them; they shall lay hands on the sick, and they shall recover. So then after the Lord had spoken unto them, he was received up into heaven, and sat on the right hand of God. And they went forth, and preached every where, the Lord working with them, and confirming the word with signs follow-ing. Amen.
>
> —Mark 16:15-20

In this passage, the word "confirm" means "remove all doubt by performing indisputable acts of authority." Today, it is the job of every Christian to remove the doubt—to perform the acts of authority!

It's time for the skeptics to be silenced. It's time for the doubters to cease. It's time for the scorners to see a God who still performs miracles.

In this book I want to show you, through God's holy Word, that the power of the anointing is available to you. The anointing can swell up out of your belly in times of adversity and propel you through every line of Satan's defense.

When you are touched by the anointing of God, you will go to places you have never been before. You will see things you have never seen before. You will do things you have never done before. Isaiah wrote,

> And it shall come to pass in that day, that his burden shall be taken away from off thy shoulder, and his yoke from off thy neck, and the yoke shall be destroyed because of the anointing.
>
> —Isaiah 10:27

The yoke Isaiah spoke of—oppression, addiction, pain, disease, hopelessness—is being destroyed because of the anointing.

At one time or another, the devil has tried to stop every person from receiving their miracle. He may be trying to stop you even now. Perhaps he is waging an all-out spiritual attack on your healing or deliverance, or on the salvation of a friend or family member.

Jesus, the Anointed One, is present to meet you at the point of your greatest need. The Gospel of Luke declares,

> And he came to Nazareth, where he had been brought up: and, as his custom was, he went into the synagogue on the sabbath day, and stood up for to read. And there was delivered unto him the book of the prophet Esaias [Isaiah]. And when he had opened the book, he found the place where it was written, The Spirit of the Lord is upon me, because he hath anointed me to preach the gospel to the poor; he hath sent me to heal the brokenhearted, to preach deliverance to the captives, and recovering

of sight to the blind, to set at liberty them that are bruised, To preach the acceptable year of the Lord.

—Luke 4:16-19

That anointing is tangible and it is transferable. The anointing of God will change you into another human being!

There is a remnant people who refuse to allow anyone or anything to stand in the way of their miracle. They refuse to be refused, and they will not be denied. Enough is enough, the time has come.

Only Jesus can heal a body. Only Jesus can touch a tormented mind. Only Jesus can put a marriage back together. Only Jesus can give a ministry back. Only Jesus can give a person joy unspeakable and full of glory. Jesus came to a hurting and desperate world in search of you.

The anointing can cool the fevered brow of an infant child. The anointing can heal a broken heart and mend a broken marriage. The anointing can transport a dying soul when life's trials and tribulations come. The anointing, through the power of the Holy Spirit, can save the most hopeless and helpless soul. The anointing can make dead things live again!

Throughout the pages of this book, I believe you will uncover God's miracle anointing for your life. You will:

- Discover how to release the tangible anointing of the Holy Spirit in your life.
- Understand how you have an impartation of the anointing through a spiritual inheritance.
- Receive your breakthrough by activating God's miracle anointing in your life.

The anointing you are looking for is not born of pomp and circumstance. It does not spring from right or ritual or religiosity. The anointing you are looking for is not found in the cadences and creeds of creation—not in the doctrines of humanity. The anointing you are looking for is not housed in a human vessel. The anointing that you are looking for comes from Christ, the Anointed One.

You must learn to walk and live in this kind of anointing. When you do, Jehovah will wrap you in robes of righteousness and crown you with crowns of glory to the point that when you walk down the street, you won't have to lay hands on anybody.

The mere shadow of your presence will make the lame get up and walk.

Maybe you have fasted long enough, prayed long enough and held on long enough. You are tired of shouting at someone else's miracle.

For too long you have gone on yesterday's anointing. Time is pregnant. Like Esther, you have come to the kingdom for such a time as this. Just like the Israelite women when Pharaoh commanded the Egyptian midwives to kill their children, you are giving birth to a miracle faster than the devil can stop you!

What is happening <u>in</u> you is greater than what is happening <u>to</u> you. You are anointed.

Have you ever been walking around with a load that seemed too heavy for you to bear? Have you ever stumbled under the weight of things you can't carry in you own human power?

Possibly you are looking for hope beyond the scope of human limitation. Maybe you are looking for a power beyond the doctors, lawyers and preachers. It is time for your yoke to be destroyed because of the anointing!

As you read this book, perhaps you will see a family member, a neighbor, a co-worker or even your own life reflected in the life of one of these ordinary people.

You may be the unlikely leader of a struggling congregation. You might be a desperate mother, a despondent father, a social outcast or just a face in the crowd. Whatever your station in life, you are about to come face to face with a loving God!

The Bible says, "The eternal God is thy refuge, and underneath are the everlasting arms: and he shall thrust out the enemy from before thee; and shall say, Destroy them" (Deuteronomy 33:27).

Jesus has seen your tears. He has felt your touch. You are not lost in the crowd. He will not leave you as He found you.

Reach out and touch Him. It's time for your need to be touched by His anointing.

Chapter One

THE UNLIKELY LEADER

And Moses said unto God, Who am I,
that I should go unto Pharaoh, and that I
should bring forth the children of Israel out
of Egypt?

—Exodus 3:11

For 400 years the Israelites had suffered in slavery in the land of Egypt. But a day came when the reigning Pharaoh did not remember the words of his forefathers concerning Joseph and his descendants. So it was during his reign that the Israelites' numbers began to increase to the point that, for fear of them, the Pharaoh commanded that all Hebrew boys be killed by the midwives who assisted in their delivery.

However, because the midwives feared God,

they conspired to thwart Pharaoh's plan. When this plot failed, Pharaoh commanded that the children be thrown into the Nile River.

Through the cunning of one Hebrew family one small boy, a deliverer, was saved. His name was Moses. The baby Moses was discovered by Pharaoh's daughter and grew up in the palace, educated in the finest of Egyptian institutions and protected by the Pharaoh himself. Even while Pharaoh was planning the extermination of the Israelites, God was planning their emancipation through the training of this unlikely leader.

One day, however, something went horribly wrong.

ON THE RUN

Though Moses was educated in the courts of Pharaoh, he still possessed a keen conscience of God. This deeply embedded standard drove him to sympathy for the suffering of his people.

Because of this Moses murdered an Egyptian who was beating one of his Hebrew brethren. Moses' love for God's chosen people also compelled him to attempt the reconciliation of two Hebrew men.

These two life-changing events drove Moses to exile in the land of Midian. There he dwelt as a stranger in a strange land, tending sheep. He must have had a lot of time to think in the fields with those sheep! And there it would be that he would meet God, forty years later.

MEETING GOD

God found Moses tending his father-in-law's sheep during this time in Midian. The Bible says,

> And the angel of the Lord appeared unto him in a flame of fire out of the midst of a bush: and he looked, and, behold, the bush burned with fire, and the bush was not consumed. And Moses said, I will now turn aside, and see this great sight, why the bush is not burnt. And when the Lord saw that he turned aside to see, God called unto him out of the midst of the bush, and said, Moses, Moses. And he said, Here am I.

And he said, Draw not nigh hither: put off thy shoes from off thy feet, for the place whereon thou standest is holy ground. Moreover he said, I am the God of thy father, the God of Abraham, the God of Isaac, and the God of Jacob. And Moses hid his face; for he was afraid to look upon God. And the Lord said, I have surely seen the affliction of my people which are in Egypt, and have heard their cry by reason of their taskmasters; for I know their sorrows.

—Exodus 3:2-7

The Lord will always find you no matter where you try to go. He wrestled with Jacob at Bethel. He knocked Saul to the ground on the road to Damascus. And even if you are running from Him today, rest assured that He will find you, too!

In Moses' mind, he was not ready for such a divine encounter. The Bible records that he was content to dwell in the land of Midian. So he presented several objections to God, pleading for Him to choose someone else to deliver His people.

Moses first asked God, essentially, "You don't

really want me, do you?" The Bible says, "And Moses said unto God, Who am I, that I should go unto Pharaoh, and that I should bring forth the children of Israel out of Egypt?" (Exodus 3:11).

Even today, it's common for God's people to consider themselves unqualified to do His work. And in a sense, they are right: no one has within themselves the capability to do what God needs to be done. But praise God, He is not limited by human capabilities! Often God, in His goodness, seeks out the least or the least likely for a task. He does this for His own purposes. Often one effect of His choices is that success through an unlikely source makes His grace appear all the more glorious.

After Saul was rejected by God as king over Israel, He sent the prophet Samuel to anoint another. God led Samuel to the house of Jesse in Bethlehem, where He told Samuel that He had chosen one of Jesse's sons to succeed Saul.

Samuel thought he had his man in Jesse's son Eliab. The Bible says,

> And it came to pass, when they were come, that he looked on Eliab, and said,

Surely the Lord's anointed is before him. But the Lord said unto Samuel, Look not on his countenance, or on the height of his stature; because I have refused him: for the Lord seeth not as man seeth; for man looketh on the outward appearance, but the Lord looketh on the heart.

—1 Samuel 16:6,7

Samuel saw all the sons Jesse presented to him, but God did not approve of any of them. One son, however, was still out in the field tending his father's sheep:

And he [Jesse] sent, and brought him [David] in. Now he was ruddy, and withal of a beautiful countenance, and goodly to look to. And the Lord said, Arise, anoint him: for this is he. Then Samuel took the horn of oil, and anointed him in the midst of his brethren: and the Spirit of the Lord came upon David from that day forward. So Samuel rose up, and went to Ramah.

—1 Samuel 16:12,13

Just think of it! The man whom God had chosen to lead a nation, though small and ruddy, was tending to the very treasure of his father's house!

God is searching for people to care for the sheep of His pasture. He is looking for men and women who, with His heart, will minister with the anointing to the needs and wounds of His flock! Just as in David's day, God looks upon the heart—the character and moral stature—of a person.

Moses, though a murderer and an exile, was just the man the Lord was looking for. He was someone whom He could mold. Because of Moses' humility, he was the very person God could use to lead His people out of bondage.

It doesn't matter what your outward appearance may look like or your abilities or lack thereof. God will anoint you for service based upon the condition of your heart.

GO IN HIS NAME

Moses then asked God if he would have His name if he agreed to step out in faith. Moses asked because he knew Pharaoh would ask the question,

"Who is the Lord that I should let this people go?" God gave a very reassuring reply: "And God said unto Moses, I AM THAT I AM: and he said, Thus shalt thou say unto the children of Israel, I AM hath sent me unto you" (Exodus 3:14).

Following God's declaration, Moses had every opportunity to go forward in confidence, because he was going forward in the name of the almighty God.

Through the anointing of the Holy Spirit I think it is time to answer the question of a scornful world and an untoward generation that asks, "Who is the Lord, that we should serve Him?" Is Buddha God, is Mohammed God or is Jesus God?

We need to be able to say with confidence: our living Lord is the reason the blind see, the deaf hear, the lame walk, the dumb speak, marriages are put back together, arthritis disappears, homes are put back together and addictions are broken. These things do not happen in the name of Mohammed. They do not happen in the name of Buddha. They can only happen when we call upon the name that is above every name—the name of Jesus!

Believe it or not, Moses had yet another objection. "And Moses answered and said, But, behold, they will not believe me, nor hearken unto my voice: for they will say, The Lord hath not appeared unto thee" (Exodus 4:1). But God already had a plan to show forth His power and anointing through mighty signs and wonders:

> And the Lord said unto him, What is that in thine hand? And he said, A rod. And he said, Cast it on the ground. And he cast it on the ground, and it became a serpent; and Moses fled from before it. And the Lord said unto Moses, Put forth thine hand, and take it by the tail. And he put forth his hand, and caught it, and it became a rod in his hand: That they may believe that the Lord God of their fathers, the God of Abraham, the God of Isaac, and the God of Jacob, hath appeared unto thee. And the Lord said furthermore unto him, Put now thine hand into thy bosom. And he put his hand into his bosom: and when he took it out, behold, his hand was leprous as snow. And he said, Put thine hand into thy bosom again. And he put his hand into his bosom again; and plucked it out of his bosom,

and, behold, it was turned again as his other flesh. And it shall come to pass, if they will not believe thee, neither hearken to the voice of the first sign, that they will believe the voice of the latter sign. And it shall come to pass, if they will not believe also these two signs, neither hearken unto thy voice, that thou shalt take of the water of the river, and pour it upon the dry land: and the water which thou takest out of the river shall become blood upon the dry land.

—Exodus 4:2-9

A sign points to something beyond itself. For example, a road sign directs you where to go. If you are among the elect of God, you are a sign. People in your spheres of influence should be able to look at you and find their way to Jesus.

A wonder is a display of the mighty acts of God that only He could accomplish. If you are among the elect of God, you are a wonder. You need to be willing and able to display the mighty works of God in your life.

Our ministry is both a sign and a wonder. When

I first began preaching, I wrote down in my Bible, "Lord, do things so incredibly great that men would have to look beyond humanity and look to God and say no man could have done this." That's a wonder.

Moses wasn't done with his objections. He was concerned that he speak appropriately for God:

> And Moses said unto the Lord, O my Lord, I am not eloquent, neither heretofore, nor since thou hast spoken unto thy servant: but I am slow of speech, and of a slow tongue. And the Lord said unto him, Who hath made man's mouth? or who maketh the dumb, or deaf, or the seeing, or the blind? have not I the Lord? Now therefore go, and I will be with thy mouth, and teach thee what thou shalt say.
>
> —Exodus 4:10-12

It is natural to want to communicate the love of God clearly. So I'm never surprised when anyone comes to me and shares that he or she feels inadequate to share the Gospel with friends and family. Would it surprise you that Jesus' disciples felt the same way? And Jesus told them, "But when they deliver you up, take no thought how or what ye shall speak: for it shall be given you in that same hour what ye shall speak" (Matthew 10:19). Likewise, the Spirit will speak through you when your resources are inadequate!

Long ago there was a preacher by the name of Uncle Bud who had stuttered his entire life. One night during a revival meeting he was preaching and a group of men arrived and sat down in the back of the tent. They had come to make fun of this stuttering man of God and disrupt the service. After several minutes of yelling and ridiculing during his sermon, one man stood up and from his pocket he removed a small, white oval object. It was an egg.

With all the force this man could muster, he threw the egg right at Uncle Bud. He didn't see it coming but right before it got to where he was standing, the anointing came upon him and he ducked, just missing the egg. He was praising God the entire time.

All of a sudden another egg came flying his way, and the same thing happened. However, this time the egg hit a leader of the church right behind him. This man, instead of praising God began to cuss. Uncle Bud said, "When the egg h-h-hit me the p-p-praise c-c-came out. When the e-e-egg h-h-hit you, what was in y-y-ou came out."

It doesn't matter if you came from the wrong side of the tracks or if you can do nothing but stutter. God knows what He has placed on the inside of you. It is called the anointing!

Finally, Moses revealed what was really on his mind: he didn't want to go! Fortunately, God was having none of it:

> And he said, O my Lord, send, I pray thee, by the hand of him whom thou wilt send. And the anger of the Lord was kindled against Moses, and he said, Is not Aaron the Levite thy brother? I know that he can speak well. And also, behold, he cometh forth to meet thee: and when he seeth thee, he will be glad in his heart. And thou shalt speak unto him, and put words in his mouth: and I will be with thy mouth, and with his mouth, and will teach you what ye shall do. And he shall be thy spokesman unto the people: and he shall be, even he shall be to thee instead of a mouth, and thou shalt be to him instead of

God. And thou shalt take this rod in thine
hand, wherewith thou shalt do signs.
—Exodus 4:13-17

Why was Moses so adamant about staying
where he was? Perhaps he sensed that he would be
scorned by his own countrymen when Pharaoh
increased their burdens. The very people he would
seek to save would ask him to leave them alone. He
had sound reasons not to obey—just like we do.

But God would not change His mind. After all
of Moses' objections were raised and all of his
inadequacies were addressed, he finally relented to
the task.

All of His life the Lord had been preparing
Moses to lead the Israelites when the moment
arrived. Although Moses could have ultimately
rejected the call of God upon him, and even tried to
do so, he finally submitted to becoming His chosen
vessel. So Moses was anointed and set aside for
this momentous time in history.

With nothing but a stick in his hand and the hot
desert sun beating against his brow, a stammering
Moses confronted Pharaoh and demanded he let the
children of God go. But Pharaoh responded arro-
gantly,

And Pharaoh said, Who is the Lord, that I should obey his voice to let Israel go? I know not the Lord, neither will I let Israel go. And they said, The God of the Hebrews hath met with us: let us go, we pray thee, three days' journey into the desert, and sacrifice unto the Lord our God; lest he fall upon us with pestilence, or with the sword. And the king of Egypt said unto them, Wherefore do ye, Moses and Aaron, let the people from their works? get you unto your burdens.

—Exodus 5:2-4

Pharaoh tried to drive the Israelites back to baking bricks, back to their burdens. This is what Satan tries to do to the body of Christ every day. He attempts to drive them, like a hard taskmaster, back to their burdens. But by the revelation of the Holy Spirit you can hear the prophetic words of the prophet Isaiah in your spirit,

And it shall come to pass in that day, that his burden shall be taken away from off thy shoulder, and his yoke from off thy neck, and the yoke shall be destroyed because of the anointing.

—Isaiah 10:27

Today, I believe it's time for depression to find out who is Lord. I think it's time for malady and malfunction to come into contact with the Lord of lords. It's time for lost children, spouses and parents to meet the King of kings!

The devil may try to tell you that you will never be free. He may try to deceive you into believing that you were destined to be bound by some burden of addiction or some negative words spoken over your life that you would never amount to anything or that your loved ones would never be saved.

But right now, as you read this book, I want you to make this statement: "It is my time for my blessing from my God!"

You serve the Anointed One. The devil will say to you, "Who is the Lord that I should let you go?" When that happens, just call on the name of Jesus—the Anointed One, the burden remover and the yoke destroyer!

I wonder how often someone has missed God's calling upon his or her life because he or she felt unable to fulfill His divine appointment in the greatest time of need? I am reminded of the Scripture,

> And I sought for a man among them, that should make up the hedge, and stand in the gap before me for the land, that I should not destroy it: but I found none.
>
> —Exekiel 22:30

God, through His anointing, will not allow you to stay where you are. He will turn you from a spectator on the sidelines of history into an instrument of revival in your family, neighborhood or city. He can transform you into an unlikely leader. He does it every day!

THE ROD OF GOD

When Moses appeared before the presence of God in the burning bush, God said to Moses, "What is in your hand?" Moses said, "It's a rod. It's just a stick." It was a shepherd's staff. It was something Moses used in his work.

God said, "Lay it down." And from that

moment on, it wasn't only known as the rod of Moses. It was known as the rod of God, and Moses used it to do supernatural things.

When God lays His hand on something and claims it as His own, He may return it to you in another form to be used for his glory, but it's never the same as it was before God took hold of it.

God claimed you for His own, but once He got a hold of you, you were never the same.

I believe there is something about your life God wants to anoint. There is a quality, a talent, a characteristic, God wants to claim as His own. Once He does, you will never be same.

There is something that God has already placed in you. Possibly He has already spoken to you about it, and it's something that He says He wants you to turn over to Him. It won't ever be the same after today, because God wants to place His hand on you in a new way—to the point where it will change you for His glory and for the eternal benefit of those with whom you come in contact.

The Lord wants to do something in your life that is going to break the yoke of bondage for you and for somebody around you. I don't know what it is. It might be speaking to somebody's unsaved relative. It might be laying hands on somebody that needs to be set free. It may be getting a financial blessing that causes you to be able to praise God in a situation in an unprecedented way. Whatever it is, it is designed to be a sign and wonder to others. It is designed to cause someone else to say, "If God can bless Him like that, maybe He can do something for me."

A MODERN-DAY MOSES

Let me share with you a testimony from a pastor who was ready to resign his church because of the onslaught of attack from the devil before he attended one of our services.

This pastor drove with a busload of members from his church. He wanted them to experience the glory of God and the power of God manifested in healing and deliverance. But inside, he was full of despair.

He was experiencing the most difficult time of his ministry. He was ready to quit and he had the resignation papers filled out laying on his desk at home. His wife felt his tremendous burden, and was crying out to God for answers.

They didn't know that God had this special

service planned for them. They thought they were just bringing their church group to receive a touch. But God also wanted to touch them. During that particular service, I called out that people who were bound by depression were being set free. I said, "You want to quit. Everyone would be surprised to hear it, but you've wanted to give up and quit." Instantly this pastor felt a heaviness leave him, and he knew the oppression was gone.

As if that wasn't enough, their daughter received a healing touch from God! She had been diagnosed with a hearing problem. The doctors said she would never be able to hear normally. After the miracle touch of healing, she was able to hear even the slightest whisper. She was tested again, and the doctors told her parents her hearing was completely normal!

COMING TO THE PROMISED LAND

After completing everything God had asked him to do to free the Hebrew people from the oppressive regime of Pharaoh, it's easy to imagine Moses nearing the end of his life leaning upon the staff which God has so mightily anointed and used in his hand to perform signs and wonders before Pharaoh and his magicians.

As the children of Israel fled, that rod stretched out over the Red Sea where the waters were divided and made a way for them to pass over. The Egyptians in turn were drowned behind them. That same staff later struck a rock which became Moses' excommunication from the promised land.

Now older and grayer, I envision Moses on the mountain of Nebo resting one last time upon that staff, as he looks toward the promised land. Forty years and many miracles later, the Lord came down to usher Moses into His pavilions of glory:

> And Moses went up from the plains of Moab unto the mountain of Nebo, to the top of Pisgah, that is over against Jericho. And the Lord shewed him all the land of Gilead, unto Dan, And all Naphtali, and the land of Ephraim, and Manasseh, and all the land of Judah, unto the utmost sea, And the south, and the plain of the valley of Jericho, the city of palm trees, unto Zoar. And the Lord said unto him, This is the

land which I sware unto Abraham, unto
Isaac, and unto Jacob, saying, I will give it
unto thy seed: I have caused thee to see it
with thine eyes, but thou shalt not go over
thither. So Moses the servant of the Lord
died there in the land of Moab, according
to the word of the Lord. And he buried him
in a valley in the land of Moab, over
against Beth-peor: but no man knoweth of
his sepulchre unto this day. And Moses
was an hundred and twenty years old when
he died: his eye was not dim, nor his natural force abated.

—Deuteronomy 34:1-7

Jehovah, who displayed Himself to Moses in
Mount Sinai, was about to meet him face to face.
God presided over the funeral of His servant
Moses. The Lord of Hosts gave the eulogy. He
buried His chosen vessel. Moses' reputation with
Israel and relationship with God had reserved him
a place in the Bible's hall of faith.

Many years later a New Testament saint wrote,

By faith Moses, when he was born,
was hid three months of his parents,

because they saw he was a proper child; and they were not afraid of the king's commandment. By faith Moses, when he was come to years, refused to be called the son of Pharaoh's daughter; Choosing rather to suffer affliction with the people of God, than to enjoy the pleasures of sin for a season; Esteeming the reproach of Christ greater riches than the treasures in Egypt: for he had respect unto the recompence of the reward. By faith he forsook Egypt, not fearing the wrath of the king: for he endured, as seeing him who is invisible. Through faith he kept the passover, and the sprinkling of blood, lest he that destroyed the firstborn should touch them. By faith they passed through the Red sea as by dry land: which the Egyptians assaying to do were drowned.

—Hebrews 11:23-29

Maybe you feel even more inadequate than Moses or the pastor I told you about. Perhaps, in your mind, you are definitely not leadership material.

Let me assure you that God wants to touch you with His anointing. Through His anointing, you will gain acceptance, ability and authority you never dreamed possible. Just as God's anointing turned a stuttering servant into a powerful leader, His anointing will transform your life.

There is one important point about a Christian leader to keep in mind. God has different tasks in mind for His leaders than the world does for its leaders! Jesus said, "And whosoever will be chief among you, let him be your servant: Even as the Son of man came not to be ministered unto, but to minister, and to give his life a ransom for many" (Matthew 20:27,28). As our Lord makes clear, the only true leaders are servants.

You may not be called to preach to the masses. You may not be selected to be a missionary in a foreign country. However, your greatest task may be, through the touch of God's anointing, to lead your family to the feet of Jesus. Perhaps you are chosen to minister to an elderly neighbor or a sick family member.

With a servant's heart, God will make you the leader you never imagined you could be.

Chapter Two

THE STEADFAST MOTHER

"Run now, I pray thee, to meet her, and say unto her, Is it well with thee? is it well with thy husband? is it well with the child? And she answered, It is well" (2 Kings 4:26).

Elisha is one of the most profound prophets of the Old Testament. He was mentored in Elijah's school of the prophets. He was a man who not only wanted what he had, but he wanted double.

Elijah was by no means a minor prophet. He raised the dead. He slew the prophets of Baal. He prayed for a drought to fall upon the land during the reign of Ahab. He even out ran Ahab's chariots when storm clouds broke over the horizon. He smote the Jordan River with his mantel and crossed over on dry ground. At the end of his earthly life, Elijah was taken up in a whirlwind in the chariot of God.

With Elijah's heavenly departure, Elisha was positioned to do twice as many miracles during his lifetime than his predecessor. Even in his death, the anointing remained in Elisha's bones, because as a dead man was cast into his open tomb and his eyes popped open and he lived again!

The anointing will cause that which was once dead to live again! It is the life force of Almighty God. The anointing will mend broken bones, broken hearts and broken dreams. The anointing will deliver the downcast and the desperate.

This next lesson, however, is not about Elijah. Instead it is about a mother who, through her steadfast faith, experienced the anointing of God in her own life.

A Chamber is Prepared

Second Kings 4 tells the story of Elisha and the Shunnamite woman. She built Elisha a little room to abide in when he came through town for revival meetings. The Bible says,

And it fell on a day, that Elisha passed

to Shunem, where was a great woman; and she constrained him to eat bread. And so it was, that as oft as he passed by, he turned in thither to eat bread. And she said unto her husband, Behold now, I perceive that this is an holy man of God, which passeth by us continually. Let us make a little chamber, I pray thee, on the wall; and let us set for him there a bed, and a table, and a stool, and a candlestick: and it shall be, when he cometh to us, that he shall turn in thither. And it fell on a day, that he came thither, and he turned into the chamber, and lay there.

—2 Kings 4:8-11

The Shunammite woman and her husband prepared a place for the man of God. It is likely that Elisha stayed there whenever he was passing through on his way to some revival meeting. In the chamber this woman furnished four things: a bed, a table, a chair and a candlestick.

Beds are for resting. The Holy Spirit has impressed upon me that the body of Christ must come to the place where the struggle ceases. The book of Hebrews says in part, "There remaineth therefore a rest to the people of God" (Hebrews 4:9).

This woman in essence said, "I am going to give this prophet a place to pillow his head and rest."

Sometimes God wants to take you to another level of His anointing, but there is a struggle taking place inside of you. God wants you to rest in Him and allow the Holy Spirit to do His perfect work in you.

Tables are for partaking of daily bread. So a table represents food or nourishment. The Shunammite woman's house was tied to God's house. She made her house Elisha's house, so that when she needed a miracle, he didn't have to ask permission. He just walked into his place. You must make a habitation for God's Spirit in your heart, through the confession of your mouth, so that when you need a miracle, He can touch you with His anointing because He is already welcome there!

If you are part of a local church, you should be able to find nourishment there. What type of nourishment should be there? Jesus said,

And these signs shall follow them that believe; In my name shall they cast out devils; they shall speak with new tongues; They shall take up serpents; and if they drink any deadly thing, it shall not hurt them; they shall lay hands on the sick, and they shall recover.

—Mark 16:17,18

If you're not being nourished in your local church, you should probably go somewhere else. But if you're growing, and if there's meat in the house, and if there's bread on the table, why in the world would you not partake of the nourishment your table is providing?

Candlesticks are for illuminating. The psalmist said, "Thy word is a lamp unto my feet, and a light unto my path" (119:105).

Chairs are for sitting. In this case, the Shunammite woman provided Elisha with a chair to give the man of God a place of authority in her life. She availed herself of his covering and protection.

The Shunammite woman continued steadfastly to serve Elisha, and her house became God's house.

While she prepared a place for Elisha, God was preparing a miracle for her.

WHAT SHALL I DO FOR THEE?

If you take care of the man of God, God will take care of you. This woman wanted a son. So Elisha prayed, and God gave her a son.

> And he said to Gehazi his servant, Call this Shunammite. And when he had called her, she stood before him. And he said unto him, Say now unto her, Behold, thou hast been careful for us with all this care; what is to be done for thee? wouldest thou be spoken for to the king, or to the captain of the host? And she answered, I dwell among mine own people. And he said, What then is to be done for her? And Gehazi answered, Verily she hath no child, and her husband is old. And he said, Call her. And when he had called her, she stood in the door. And he said, About this season, according to the time of life, thou shalt

embrace a son. And she said, Nay, my lord, thou man of God, do not lie unto thine handmaid. And the woman conceived, and bare a son at that season that Elisha had said unto her, according to the time of life.

—2 Kings 4:12-17

Wouldn't most of us long for God just to walk up and ask us, "What do you want?"

Let me paraphrase this passage of Scripture for you. Elisha said, "About this time next year you will hold your own child. It is your time!" Did you notice that it was not the right season until she set everything in order? But when she set everything in order, it became her season.

The woman replied, "Don't you lie to me!" Perhaps she had longed for a son for many years and had given up hope that motherhood would become part of her life. Sometimes God's promises seem too good to be true. You may say, "Oh, God, don't say that to me. I'll only get my hopes up." But as the psalmist said, "When the Lord turned again the captivity of Zion, we were like them that dream. Then was our mouth filled with laughter, and our tongue with singing: then said they among the heathen, The Lord hath done great things for them" (Psalm 126:1,2).

THE MIRACLE DIES

True to Elisha's word, the woman's miracle child was born. But tragically, one day the boy collapsed and died. A mother's hopes were devastated by an unexpected turn of events:

> And when the child was grown, it fell on a day, that he went out to his father to the reapers. And he said unto his father, My head, my head. And he said to a lad, Carry him to his mother. And when he had taken him, and brought him to his mother, he sat on her knees till noon, and then died. And she went up, and laid him on the bed of the man of God, and shut the door upon him, and went out.
>
> —2 Kings 4:18-21

While my mentor and pastor, Dr. Lester Sumrall, was living, he would stay in our home while he was ministering at our church. We would try to get him the finest suite in the most beautiful hotel in town. But he wouldn't stay there.

One time in particular I asked him, "Why do you not want to go to that hotel when they've got room service and everything?" He said, "One reason. I want to sleep in your bed."

He didn't want to sleep in my bed to get what I had. He wanted to sleep in my bed to leave what he had—an impartation of the anointing!

After Dr. Sumrall visited us I would tell my wife, Joni, "Just leave those sheets alone. We're going to sleep in the anointing tonight!"

The Shunammite woman's son lay lifeless in the room that had been prepared for the man of God. The child of promise was now dead.

> And she called unto her husband, and said, Send me, I pray thee, one of the young men, and one of the asses, that I may run to the man of God, and come again. And he said, Wherefore wilt thou go to him to day? it is neither new moon, nor sabbath. And she said, It shall be well.
>
> —2 Kings 4:22,23

Notice that the woman said it shall be well. It wasn't well yet because her child was still dead. She didn't even tell her husband that the boy had died. She went to what she knew would be the boy's source of healing.

> Then she saddled an ass, and said to her servant, Drive, and go forward; slack not thy riding for me, except I bid thee. So she went and came unto the man of God to mount Carmel. And it came to pass, when the man of God saw her afar off, that he said to Gehazi his servant, Behold, yonder is that Shunammite: Run now, I pray thee, to meet her, and say unto her, Is it well with thee? is it well with thy husband? is it well with the child? And she answered, It is well. And when she came to the man of God to the hill, she caught him by the feet: but Gehazi came near to thrust her away. And the man of God said, Let her alone; for her soul is vexed within her: and the Lord hath hid it from me, and hath not told me. Then she said, Did I desire a son of my lord? did I not say, Do not deceive me?

Then he said to Gehazi, Gird up thy loins, and take my staff in thine hand, and go thy way: if thou meet any man, salute him not; and if any salute thee, answer him not again: and lay my staff upon the face of the child. And the mother of the child said, As the Lord liveth, and as thy soul liveth, I will not leave thee. And he arose, and followed her. And Gehazi passed on before them, and laid the staff upon the face of the child; but there was neither voice, nor hearing. Wherefore he went again to meet him, and told him, saying, The child is not awaked.

—2 Kings 4:24-31

Note that Elisha said, "Is it well with thee?" And she replied, "It is well."

He said, "Is it well with thy husband?" And she said, "It is well."

Then Elisha said, "Is it well with thy son?" And the woman replied, "All is well." Yet her son was dead, laying on the man of God's bed.

The Shunammite woman went to meet the man of God with an expectant spirit. She was about to make a withdrawal on the deposit she had made into Elisha, the prophet of God. The atmosphere of expectancy is the breeding ground of miracles.

IT IS WELL

There is a story told of a Presbyterian layman from Chicago named Horatio G. Spafford, who was a successful businessman and a noted gospel musician. However, tragedy struck during the great Chicago fire of 1871. Some months prior, Mr. Spafford had secured great investments in real estate. All of them were destroyed during this disaster.

Desiring a rest for his wife and four daughters as well as wishing to assist D.L. Moody and Sankey in one of their campaigns in Great Britain, Spafford planned a European trip for his family in November of 1873. Due to unexpected last-minute business developments, he had to remain in Chicago, but he sent his wife and four daughters on ahead as scheduled on the S.S. Ville du Havre. He expected to follow in a few days.

On November 22 the ship was struck by the

Lochearn, an English vessel, and sank. Several days later the survivors finally landed at Cardiff, Wales, and Mrs. Spafford cabled her husband, 'Saved alone.'

Shortly afterward Spafford left by ship to join his bereaved wife. It is thought that on the sea near the area where his four daughters drowned, Spafford penned a text to describe his grief. You've sung these words:

"When peace like a river, attendeth my way, When sorrows like sea billows roll. Whatever my lot, Thou hast taught me to say, It is well, it is well with my soul."

Something told the Shunammite woman that if she could just get to the man of God, everything would be alright. The Spirit of the Lord revealed to Elisha that there was something wrong with the boy. He told his servant Gehazi, to take his staff and and lay it upon him.

He took his staff, laid it on the boy, however, nothing happened. He brought back the report that the child was still dead.

PERSONAL CONTACT

Sometimes your miracle needs personal contact. Sometimes the intern can't fix what an experienced doctor can. Sometimes you don't need to call a healing line. You need the personal touch of the Master, Jesus Christ.

That is what Kathleen from Tulsa needed. When the Lord led her to request a prayer cloth from our Breakthrough ministry, she had no idea she would find a lump on her breast a short time later. When she discovered the lump, she immediately claimed her healing and pinned the cloth to her clothing. The lump was gone within days!

The Shunammite woman demanded personal contact from Elisha. Why? Perhaps she discerned that his servant, Gehazi was a petty thief and a hypocrite. For later, Elisha would discover him trying to swindle Namaan, the leper of his clothes and money. Regardless, this woman was not leaving until she her son was restored to life:

> And when Elisha was come into the house, behold, the child was dead, and laid upon his bed. He went in therefore, and

shut the door upon them twain, and prayed unto the Lord. And he went up, and lay upon the child, and put his mouth upon his mouth, and his eyes upon his eyes, and his hands upon his hands: and he stretched himself upon the child; and the flesh of the child waxed warm. Then he returned, and walked in the house to and fro; and went up, and stretched himself upon him: and the child sneezed seven times, and the child opened his eyes. And he called Gehazi, and said, Call this Shunammite. So he called her. And when she was come in unto him, he said, Take up thy son.

—2 Kings 4:32-36

Have you ever had a miracle die? This woman's boy died, and she took him and laid him on the bed of Elisha. Elisha went up and lay upon the child and put his mouth upon his mouth, his eyes upon his eyes and his hands upon his hands, and he stretched himself upon the child. However, he was just getting warm.

Then the Bible says, Elisha laid on him again and breathed into him. He was not about to give up and let this promised son die.

I believe the book of Hebrews pays tribute to this steadfast mother and her faith where it says, "Women received their dead raised to life again" (Hebrews 11:35a).

Years later, after displaying God's miracle anointing by raising the woman's son to life, Elisha died. The Bible proclaims,

> And Elisha died, and they buried him. And the bands of the Moabites invaded the land at the coming in of the year. And it came to pass, as they were burying a man, that, behold, they spied a band of men; and they cast the man into the sepulchre of Elisha: and when the man was let down, and touched the bones of Elisha, he revived, and stood up on his feet.
>
> —2 Kings 13:20,21

Can you imagine? Elijah's old dead, bleached bones were laying in a cave. An army came by. They were being pursued by their enemy and didn't have time to even bury their dead. Instead they cast the body of a young soldier into a cave. I can only imagine that part of his body was laying on some rocks. Some might have been laying in a pool of water. And, perhaps just a finger touched one of Elisha's bones.

All of a sudden, something started shooting out of the bones and into the dead finger. The hand started shaking. His arm, legs and body began to tremble. He was alive!

Why? Because the anointing is transferable and the anointing is tangible!

Today you may feel the weight of the anointing coming upon you, because the devil tried to move you out. He attempted to trick you. He worked to get you to run off and leave your dream. Possibly he told you there wasn't a place for you.

There comes a time in your life when enough is enough. There comes a time when you must draw a line in the spiritual sand and tell the devil you are taking back what rightfully belongs to you. Now is the time to lift your hands and allow God's anointing to come upon you. With the same faith of this steadfast mother, don't allow yourself to be left out of the blessing of God for your life!

Chapter Three

THE SOCIAL OUTCAST

Several years ago, I attended a conference with the late Dr. Lester Sumrall, at Oral Roberts University in Tulsa, Oklahoma. There were more than 8,000 men and women in attendance. We were seated over against a curtain on two folding chairs near the front of the platform. I don't remember who the guest speaker was that particular evening, but the events that transpired in the next few moments made an impact on my life forever.

Brother Sumrall reached over and put my hand on his belly, and he said, "Do you feel that?"

I had to confess that I did. It was as though something was leaping on the inside of his belly. Dr. Sumrall said, "That's the healing anointing. Dr. Oral Roberts is somewhere in this building."

I said, "Pastor, he's scheduled to be out of the state. He's not here." Then Dr. Sumrall squeezed my knee to let me know that he was trying to teach me something. He said, "It doesn't matter to me where they say he is. My spirit tells me that anointing is here."

At that moment, a hand squeezed the back of my neck and shook hands with my pastor. Dr. Oral Roberts proceeded to walk to the platform, interrupt the speaker, and said, "The healing anointing is here."

I believe that even as you read this book, the anointing is available where you are to heal, deliver and restore whatever is broken in your life or in your family!

THE LORD IS PASSING BY

There is the story in the Bible of a woman who was an outcast for twelve years. It is the narrative of a social misfit who wasn't even allowed to be with her family or friends. The Gospel of Mark records it this way:

And Jesus went with him; and much people followed him, and thronged him. And a certain woman, which had an issue of blood twelve years, And had suffered many things of many physicians, and had spent all that she had, and was nothing bettered, but rather grew worse, When she had heard of Jesus, came in the press behind, and touched his garment.

For she said, If I may touch but his clothes, I shall be whole. And straightway the fountain of her blood was dried up; and she felt in her body that she was healed of that plague. And Jesus, immediately knowing in himself that virtue had gone out of him, turned him about in the press, and said, Who touched my clothes? And his disciples said unto him, Thou seest the multitude thronging thee, and sayest thou, Who touched me? And he looked round about to see her that had done this thing. But the woman fearing and trembling, knowing what was done in her, came and fell down before him, and told him all the truth.

And he said unto her, Daughter, thy faith hath made thee whole; go in peace, and be whole of thy plague.

—Mark 5:24-34

Jesus was traveling from place to place ministering to the needs of people. Before entering this town he had been to the other side of Galilee, casting out a legion of devils from a man who was possessed. Today, however, Jesus was on His way to the home of Jairus, a ruler of the synagogue, to minister to his sick daughter (we'll talk about him in the next chapter).

En route, a crowd gathered around Him. He could barely move. Women lifted their children up to try to get a glimpse of Jesus. Strong men tried to push their way through the crowd, so that their eyes could meet His.

Augustine said, "Flesh presses, but faith touches." People today are no different. Some seek Jesus because they are curious. Some of them are among the crowd because they are looking to see somebody else. But God knows the difference.

Jesus never looked upon a gathering of people

as a mob. Each person in the crowd, he knew intimately and personally.

There are those who can look Him in the eye and never see Him. There are those who can jostle His clothes and never feel Him. There are those that can listen to His voice but never hear Him. But praise God, you don't have to be one of those people. You can see, feel and hear the living Lord! You just need to be open to His presence.

WHO IS HE?

Jesus had heard who the world thought He was. He then approached His disciples:

> When Jesus came into the coasts of Caesarea Philippi, he asked his disciples, saying, Whom do men say that I the Son of man am? And they said, Some say that thou art John the Baptist: some, Elias; and others, Jeremias, or one of the prophets. He saith unto them, But whom say ye that I am? And Simon Peter answered and said,

Thou art the Christ, the Son of the living God. And Jesus answered and said unto him, Blessed art thou, Simon Barjona: for flesh and blood hath not revealed it unto thee, but my Father which is in heaven. And I say also unto thee, That thou art Peter, and upon this rock I will build my church; and the gates of hell shall not prevail against it. And I will give unto thee the keys of the kingdom of heaven: and whatsoever thou shalt bind on earth shall be bound in heaven: and whatsoever thou shalt loose on earth shall be loosed in heaven.

—Matthew 13:16-19

Peter saw through the eyes of the Spirit exactly who Jesus was and He made the announcement, "thou art the Christ." The word Christ actually translates "the Anointed One."

Peter knew Jesus was not only anointed to, in Jesus' own words, heal the brokenhearted, preach deliverance to the captives and deliverance to them who are bruised. Peter knew in his heart that Jesus was "the Anointed One," God Himself wrapped in humanity. All power in heaven and earth was given unto Him because He was the Son of Man.

Why then did God have to anoint Jesus, His only Son? The apostle Paul wrote that Jesus "who, being in the form of God, thought it not robbery to be equal with God: But made himself of no reputation, and took upon him the form of a servant, and was made in the likeness of men" (Philippians 2:6,7).

Jesus did not heal and deliver people because He was the Son of God. Jesus was anointed because He was the Son of Man. God, being a Spirit, cannot do anything without a body, because a spirit has no authority in this earth. The Gospel of John bears this out:

> Verily, verily, I say unto you, He that entereth not by the door into the sheepfold, but climbeth up some other way, the same is a thief and a robber. But he that entereth in by the door is the shepherd of the sheep.
> —John 10:1,2

Travel with me to the city upon a hill. It's a hot day. The Palestinian sun is beating down on the cobblestone streets of Jerusalem. There's a crowd. Dust is everywhere. Jesus is passing by.

Some declare He's a prophet. Others say He's a madman. One man said, "All I know is that I was blind, and now I see."

Good news travels swiftly. It rang in the ears of blind Bartimaeus. He heard that Jesus was passing by. Zaccheus climbed up in a sycamore tree, because he heard that Jesus was passing by.

Now imagine that you can see the woman in the Gospel of Mark whose story you just read. She was not someone who decided to show up in the crowd to see what the Master would do for someone else. She did not come to be a cheerleader at another person's miracle. She did not even come to be seen. She approached Jesus behind, so she could not be seen.

This woman was a social outcast. She may have been abused. She may have been promiscuous. It really doesn't matter. But it's very likely that she had often said to herself, "I'm to blame for my condition."

She is tired. The stench on that hot day permeated the atmosphere around her. People screamed out, "Unclean!"

According to Hebrew law she was not permitted to touch another person. For twelve years she was excommunicated from the fellowship of the saints. By law she was separated from her husband and children. For twelve lonely years she suffered the stigma of living just out of reach—and out of touch—of another person.

It had been twelve years since anyone had brushed her hair back from her face. It had been twelve years since she felt the warmth of a handshake or the love of an embrace. She had spent everything she had just to try to rid herself of the debilitating disease that kept her all alone. And the doctors had not been able to heal her. In fact, their primitive treatments made her condition even worse! You can imagine the despair she must have felt.

Now this woman was thin and emaciated from the slow toll this disease had taken upon her. She had heard other testimonies and now faith was beginning to spring up within her.

There will come a time when you will give anything for one moment's relief from your pain. This woman knew that feeling, and she needed hope beyond the scope of human limitation.

THE NEWS OF JESUS' MIRACLES

There were four things this woman did in this narrative. First, she heard Jesus was in town. She may have heard the stories of the multitudes Jesus had healed from town to town. Perhaps she heard the story of blind Bartimaeus. Maybe one of her relatives shared with her the wonderful display of compassion and deliverance toward the young child who often cast himself into the fire. Whatever she had heard, it stirred her to the very depths of her spirit to believe this man, the carpenter's son, could heal her also.

Can you see this little woman bent over? She heard the good news that Jesus was passing by. She had a decision to make. She could discard her faith and give up, or she could direct her faith and be lifted up.

She had a choice to make. She could let her mountain move her faith, or she could let her faith move her mountain. She determined that she not only had faith, she had faith to pursue.

The proof of desire is in pursuit. If you want your miracle bad enough, there's nothing that can stand in your way. If you desire the Master's touch, it doesn't matter what anyone says about you. It doesn't matter what another person thinks about you.

Possibly you could care less about anybody else, because there isn't anyone else who can help you out of your situation. So with dogged determination, you declare within yourself, "I don't care what anyone else thinks. I have to get to Jesus!"

SHE SPOKE TO HERSELF

Second, she spoke to herself. She said within herself, "If I can touch the hem of His garment, I know I will be made whole."

Faith will cause you to talk to yourself. The apostle Paul wrote, "For with the heart man believeth unto righteousness; and with the mouth confession is made unto salvation" (Romans 10:10).

At the same time the woman with the issue of blood was healed, others were there who experienced Jesus' touch. The Bible says,

And when they had passed over, they came into the land of Gennesaret, and drew to the shore. And when they were come out of the ship, straightway they knew him, And ran through that whole region round about, and began to carry about in beds those that were sick, where they heard he was. And whithersoever he entered, into villages, or cities, or country, they laid the sick in the streets, and besought him that they might touch if it were but the border of his garment: and as many as touched him were made whole.

—Mark 6:53-56

You don't need another preacher. You need Jesus. Your family doesn't need another doctor. They need Jesus. Your friend doesn't need another counselor. They need Jesus' healing, delivering, saving touch.

This woman whose body was wrecked with an issue of blood began to say within herself, or she began to rehearse within her spirit, words of faith.

Humility and embarrassment demanded that she share it with no one. She was wrapped and draped in rags and hiding behind the crowd. She stretched with all her might just to touch the hem of His garment.

There are some things you just can't talk to anybody about. Her situation couldn't be told to anyone.

God wants to set every person free from the very thing that they cannot share with another soul. Perhaps you are that person.

I am not referring to the testimony you tell everybody. I am talking about that thing that you can't tell anyone, possibly not even your family. I am talking about that thing that makes you walk the floor at night. I am talking about that thing you can't even share with your pastor.

As this woman began to talk inside herself, it was as though a painter was beginning to paint a picture on the canvas of her soul. The longer he continued to paint, the clearer the image became.

This is what happens on the inside of you when you begin to say, "If I can just touch Him, I know I'll be made whole."

You can't see it and, at first it doesn't seem real. In the beginning you don't think it's ever going to happen, but you just keep speaking to yourself.

And, the more you say it, the more the Holy Spirit anoints it. Then God, Himself, takes His Word, and on the canvas of your life He begins to paint an image of you delivered, healed and set free!

The prophet Jeremiah saw once something out of the ordinary:

> Moreover the word of the Lord came unto me, saying, Jeremiah, what seest thou? And I said, I see a rod of an almond tree. Then said the Lord unto me, Thou hast well seen: for I will hasten my word to perform it.
>
> —Jeremiah 1:11,12

What was God saying in this passage of Scripture? First let me point out what the writer of Hebrews said, "By him therefore let us offer the sacrifice of praise to God continually, that is, the fruit of our lips giving thanks to his name" (Hebrews 13:15).

Don't think God has forsaken you in the middle of your winter of the tragedy of your life. Stand your ground.

In Jeremiah and Hebrews, our Heavenly Father

was saying, in the middle of the winter of your life, lift up your head, lift up your hands and from a heart filled with faith, begin to declare, "I shall be made whole." The fruit of your lips will be the attraction, and the Lord will run to His Word, and He will perform it.

The woman with the issue of blood did not have her healing yet but she said "I shall be made whole."

Jesus said,

> And Jesus answering saith unto them, Have faith in God. For verily I say unto you, That whosoever shall say unto this mountain, Be thou removed, and be thou cast into the sea; and shall not doubt in his heart, but shall believe that those things which he saith shall come to pass; he shall have whatsoever he saith. Therefore I say unto you, What things soever ye desire, when ye pray, believe that ye receive them, and ye shall have them.
>
> —Mark 11:22-24

Believing that God will do a great work in your

life is essential. What can the devil do with you when he comes to you and says, "You don't have your healing," and you respond, "I shall!" He may say, "Your marriage is a mess." You answer, "But I shall have restoration." If you are with addiction, you can know you shall be set free. The devil can't do anything when somebody has their faith zeroed in on the "I shall have it!"

FAITH TOUCHED HIM

Third, this woman touched the hem of His garment. The definition of touch in this scripture is the Greek word "hepto" which means "to take hold of." She did not just brush by Jesus. As Jacob wrestled with the angel at the brook at Jabbock all night, this woman took hold of God. She grabbed hold of Jesus with pit-bull faith.

They tried to beat her away, but she grabbed that purple thread in the bottom of His garment, because she understood transference. He became her scapegoat.

In the old covenant, one goat was killed on the day of atonement, but there was another called the scapegoat. The priest took his hands and dipped them in blood, and put the blood on the scapegoat. The Bible records that the animal was then taken out into an uninhabited place.

This woman wasn't just trying to receive something from Jesus. She had something on her that she wanted to put on Him—a life-ravaging disease.

Fourth, this woman with the issue of blood felt healing come in and sickness go out! Once she touched the border of Jesus' garment, she was immediately set free! How wonderful one touch can be.

Once this woman received her healing, she hoped to slip back into the crowd and be on her way. However, Jesus called her out: "And he said unto her, Daughter, thy faith hath made thee whole; go in peace, and be whole of thy plague" (Mark 5:34).

Jesus doesn't heal just part way. Though healed, this woman was still excommunicated from the temple, still separated from her husband, still ostracized by her friends. However, Jesus adopted her. He met her conscious need, but He didn't stop there. He totally restored the woman's life!

Jesus is waiting to restore in your life whatever

most needs restoring. The apostle Paul wrote,

> According as he hath chosen us in him before the foundation of the world, that we should be holy and without blame before him in love: Having predestinated us unto the adoption of children by Jesus Christ to himself, according to the good pleasure of his will, To the praise of the glory of his grace, wherein he hath made us accepted in the beloved. In whom we have redemption through his blood, the forgiveness of sins, according to the riches of his grace.
>
> —Ephesians 1:4-7

New life began for this woman, both physically and spiritually! She no longer had to stand off at a distance as a social outcast. She was now God's child!

DELIVERED BY GOD'S POWER

Not long ago the parents of a backslidden daughter, named Chrissy, wrote to our ministry requesting a prayer cloth. Chrissy had been running from the Lord and was deep into the partying, drugs and alcohol scene. Her only friends were those steeped in this same lifestyle.

After receiving the prayer cloth, Chrissy's parents began to see immediate results. First, Chrissy's brother begged her to attend a revival service with him. However, when she arrived the revival was over. The devil had convinced her that she was so bad, she couldn't change.

Everyone in town talked about her. But one day she attended another service in which the pastor ministered about the Samaritan woman. It was as though the pastor was talking directly to her, and she felt the power of God break the bondage of Satan in her life.

Two months after Crissy's parents placed the cloth on her picture, she was back home serving the Lord!

TELL THE DEVIL 'SHUT UP'

Jesus came into this earth stripped of His divinity and clothed in humanity so that He could show you how you could display your authority, through the anointing, over the devil.

The Gospel of Luke portrays a wonderful example of Jesus displaying the anointing as the Son of man. The physician wrote,

> And he arose out of the synagogue, and entered into Simon's house. And Simon's wife's mother was taken with a great fever; and they besought him for her. And he stood over her, and rebuked the fever; and it left her: and immediately she arose and ministered unto them. Now when the sun was setting, all they that had any sick with divers diseases brought them unto him; and he laid his hands on every one of them, and healed them. And devils also came out of many, crying out, and saying, Thou art Christ the Son of God. And he rebuking them suffered them not to speak: for they knew that he was Christ.
> —Luke 4:38-41

Not only is the devil a thief and a robber, he is a liar. He tried to stop Jesus from performing miracles by declaring Him to be the Son of God when He was walking this earth and anointed as the Son of Man. Jesus' response was simply, "Shut up!" We need to tell the devil to "Shut up!" in our lives as well!

REACH OUT AND TOUCH THE LORD

In the gospel of Luke, Jesus set the Pharisees straight about the impact of His words.

> And the Pharisees also, who were covetous, heard all these things: and they derided him. And he said unto them, Ye are they which justify yourselves before men; but God knoweth your hearts: for that which is highly esteemed among men is abomination in the sight of God. The law and the prophets were until John: since that time the kingdom of God is preached, and every man presseth into it. And it is easier for heaven and earth to pass, than one tittle of the law to fail.
>
> —Luke 16:14-17

This is the day and this is the hour when you will no longer have to wait for a shadow to touch and heal us. You will force your way to receive whatever it is you need from Jesus!

Like the woman with the issue of blood, with the anointing you must press forward, press into and press through until you reach Jesus and take hold of His miracle-working power. You may be buffeted and beaten back, but you must not turn away!

On the way to raise the dead, she could have said, "My problem is too small compared to Jairus' daughter. She's already dead. Perhaps I shouldn't trouble the Master. There is more than enough room at the Master's table."

There is that touch that makes a demand on His anointing. There is that touch that will not let go. There is that wrestling that says, "You cannot go until you bless me."

Jesus wants you to cast all of your care on Him. Touch Him and let it go. He's passing by this moment with a tangible anointing. I love that old song which says,

"Reach out and touch the Lord as He goes by. You will find He's not too busy to hear your heart's cry. He is passing by this moment your needs to supply. Reach out and touch the Lord as He goes by."

You've prayed long enough, hoped long enough and believed long enough. The Bible says,

> For he saith, I have heard thee in a time accepted, and in the day of salvation have I succoured thee: behold, now is the accepted time; behold, now is the day of salvation.
>
> —2 Corinthians 6:2

Today is your day! Can you sense His presence? He is not some ghostly being far removed from you. He is with you right now as you read this book!

You don't have to be lost in this crowd. Jesus is passing by!

Chapter Four

THE ONLY CHILD

My pastor was a great friend of one of the greatest apostles that ever graced this planet. His name was Smith Wigglesworth.

Brother Wigglesworth was staying in a home conducting a revival meeting in London. He had been there for several weeks when it came time for the meeting to end and for him to move on to the next one.

In the home in which he had been staying, the wife was saved but the husband was not. The day Brother Wigglesworth was to leave and began walking down the front steps, the woman threw the screen door open and she said, "Brother Wigglesworth! You can't' leave!"

He looked at his watch and said, "Madam, it's

time for me to go. I have a meeting in another city."

She began to weep and she said, "You can't leave! My husband is not yet saved. He's an alcoholic, and he's not serving God. I don't want him to go to hell."

Let me just interject this here: When the vessel leaves, the anointing remains like a residue.

Brother Wigglesworth turned around and said, "No problem, just don't change the sheets." He had been sleeping in their bed. He had been praying in their bed. God had been there and when He has been there, you don't have to ask anybody. You know God is in the place.

Jesus had just arrived back in the city of Capernaum after a short ministry trip to the country of the Gaderenes. While there he cast a legion of demons from a man who dwelt among the caves. This was not the first time he had commanded the devil to free a possessed person.

Now, however, Jesus was about to resume His Father's work in His own home town, which was also the home of Peter, Andrew, James, John and Matthew. Here he would confront the sting of death.

This city was the location of more miracles than any other in the world. It was to this place that the multitudes brought their sick and feeble. It was to this site that the diseased were laid at Jesus' feet.

This was where the blind received their sight, beholding the wonderful face of their Savior. It was where the deaf heard the sound of Jesus' voice for the first time. It was where the limbs of lame men and women were straightened. It was where the insane were returned to their right mind. It was where epileptics were healed of the seizures which struck their bodies. It was where the possessed were unloosed from the confines of the devil's bondage. It was where the chains of sin were broken by the anointing upon prostitutes and tax collectors.

But on this occasion, an even greater miracle was about to occur—the resurrection of the dead. The Bible says,

> And when Jesus was passed over again by ship unto the other side, much people gathered unto him: and he was nigh unto the sea. And, behold, there cometh one of the rulers of the synagogue, Jairus by

name; and when he saw him, he fell at his feet, And besought him greatly, saying, My little daughter lieth at the point of death: I pray thee, come and lay thy hands on her, that she may be healed; and she shall live. And Jesus went with him; and much people followed him, and thronged him.

—Mark 5:21-24

HE WILL AWAKEN

As we see from this passage of Scripture, Jairus was a ruler of one of the synagogues. However, with tremendous reverence and humility, though a religious leader, he fell at Jesus' feet.

Jairus came personally to Jesus amidst the crowd to beg Him greatly to cure his only daughter. He bid Him come and lay his hands upon her and rescue her from the grave. Just as the centurion honored Jesus as a man in authority, so Jairus esteemed Him as one greater than himself. For he knew that nowhere else could he obtain the mercy and miracle he so desperately needed. He needed just one touch of the anointing.

It is important to note that the name Jairus

means "he will awaken." Names during Biblical times held great significance. The name Jesus Christ, for instance, meant "the anointing which breaks every yoke." Can you imagine Jairus' mother the day he was born? Possibly he aroused her soul and, the joy of his birth, awakened her to new life. Today, however, death had darkened Jairus' heart and deprived him of the honor of his name. Despondency of spirit over his dying daughter drove him to desperation.

Jairus was a desperate man in search of drastic measures. However, God was preparing his heart through a seemingly insignificant series of events to receive his child to life again.

Jairus ran all the way from his home to meet the Master. His twelve-year-old daughter was lying at home, dying. He didn't have time for church. He needed a miracle. He didn't have time for a theological discourse. His daughter needed touched by the anointing.

Jairus was in a hurry and all of a sudden Jesus stopped in mid-step. Can you imagine what happened to him?

Out of nowhere Jesus said, "Who touched me?" From the last chapter, we are familiar with the story of how the woman with the issue of blood was healed.

Jesus passed through the throng to the house of Jairus, to raise the ruler's dead daughter. But in His goodness, He performs another miracle along the way. There was enough anointing to heal both the woman with the issue of blood and Jairus' daughter. I like to say that the anointing is like a fragrance which attracts the blessing and favor of God.

Jesus' anointing not only reaches its ordained target, but also enriches the air around Him. Virtue flows from Jesus, like a sweet-smelling aroma from spring flowers. If Jesus is ready to heal the sick and deliver the oppressed, then do not hesitate to put yourself in His path. The anointing is bountiful, and it only takes one touch.

Why was this woman's story important to Jairus? Jesus didn't stop and ask the question, "Who touched me?" because He didn't know who stopped Him. It was that little old woman—the social outcast. She probably didn't know anything about church. In fact, she had a disease which caused her to have an issue of blood for twelve years. She had been ostracized from society for twelve years; may have been divorced from her husband; and possibly was excommunicated from the fellowship of the saints. It's likely that for twelve long and lonely years, she walked the streets with people yelling, "Unclean!" at her.

But, she thought, "I'll just slip in. I'll get my blessing and run."

However, Jesus demanded, "Who touched me?" His disciples must have laughed. They said, "Everybody's touching you." But Jesus responded, "Someone touched me differently, because I perceive that virtue has gone out of Me."

What is virtue? It is power. Virtue is the anointing that will break every yoke of bondage. It is the power to propel you through every line of Satan's defense!

Just moments earlier, she was unclean and bleeding. The stench was sickening, but one touch from the Anointed One changed all of that.

Did you ever wonder why Jesus didn't proceed to Jairus house? After all, the woman received her healing. She didn't want any attention drawn to herself anyway.

Why didn't Jesus just go on? Because Jesus wanted Jairus to witness the miraculous. I think Jesus must have detected a little doubt in Jairus' heart, so He stopped. Then Jesus turned to the woman with the issue of blood and said, "Come here, little lady, and testify."

All of a sudden this little woman began to share the tragedy and trials of her life. She began to confess how for twelve long, lonely years no one wanted to touch her. On this day, however, she came not to be touched by someone but, rather, to touch Someone.

I can almost see the look of anxiety and impatience upon Jairus' face. All of a sudden while Jesus was ministering to that woman, some of Jairus' servants came with a bad report.

YOUR ONLY CHILD IS DEAD

A few people came and told Jairus, "Don't trouble Him any longer. It's over. Your girl is dead."

> While he [Jesus] yet spake, there came from the ruler of the synagogue's house certain which said, Thy daughter is dead: why troublest thou the Master any further?
> —Mark 5:35

But then Jairus began to hear that little woman testify, and every time she would say, "for twelve years," something would begin to leap inside of him.

I think Jairus began to remember, "The moment this woman moved under the darkness of exile was the morning my dream child was born like the dawning of a new day. My little girl was born and she fulfilled the totality of my name. My soul was awakened.

"For twelve years this woman had trudged through life with everything going wrong, and for twelve years I have experienced joy unspeakable and full of glory. I have known the warmth of my daughter's hugs and the sweetness of her kisses."

Then Jairus heard this woman say, "When I touched Him I was made whole."

You don't need a preacher. You just need Jesus. You don't need another healing service. You just need the hem of His garment!

Jesus made the woman with the issue of blood testify for three reasons. First, through her confession, this woman would have to come into direct relationship with Him. For too long, the body of Christ has just wanted to grab a blessing and run away.

The apostle Paul wrote,

> That if thou shalt confess with thy mouth the Lord Jesus, and shalt believe in thine heart that God hath raised him from the dead, thou shalt be saved. For with the heart man believeth unto righteousness; and with the mouth confession is made unto salvation.
>
> —Romans 10:9,10

The second reason this woman needed to certify her miracle was because Jairus's faith needed to be strengthened. The Bible says, "So then faith cometh by hearing, and hearing by the word of God" (Romans 10:17). Jairus needed to know that if Jesus could heal her, He could surely heal his daughter.

Finally, Jesus made her testify because He wanted to glorify the Father through her miracle. The apostle John stated the importance of testifying to the miracle working power of Jesus when he wrote, "And they overcame him by the blood of the Lamb, and by the word of their testimony; and they loved not their lives unto the death" (Revelation 12:11).

ONLY BELIEVE

Jairus had heard the worst news of his life. But Jesus sought immediately to comfort him:

"As soon as Jesus heard the word that was spoken, he saith unto the ruler of the synagogue, Be not afraid, only believe" (Mark 5:36).

Oswald Chambers once said, "Death cancels everything but truth." Jesus will hold you when your world seems to be crashing around you. Take this testimony, for example:

Walter and Nancy were believing for a healing for their son, Joey. Not long ago they wrote to our ministry:

"Joey is ten years old and watches *Breakthrough* faithfully everyday. Joey was born three months premature and, as a result, has a condition called cerebral palsy. He is currently in a wheelchair. His prayer is that the Lord will heal him completely.

"A few years ago, friends attended Dominion Camp Meeting. They brought back a prayer cloth and placed it on Joey. A few weeks later, we noticed that his one leg that was shorter than the other had grown. It grew so much that the shoe lift he had was taken down by several inches.

"Our prayer and Joey's prayer is for a complete and total healing, so he would never have to be in a wheelchair again."

Jesus only asked one thing of Jairus—that he believe. Isaiah 41:10 says, "Fear thou not; for I am with thee: be not dismayed; for I am thy God: I will strengthen thee; yea, I will help thee; yea, I will uphold thee with the right hand of my righteousness."

She Is Only Asleep

And he suffered no man to follow him, save Peter, and James, and John the brother of James. And he cometh to the house of the ruler of the synagogue, and seeth the tumult, and them that wept and wailed greatly. And when he was come in, he saith unto them, Why make ye this ado, and weep? the damsel is not dead, but sleepeth. And they laughed him to scorn. But when he had put them all out, he taketh the father

and the mother of the damsel, and them
that were with him, and entereth in where
the damsel was lying.

—Mark 5:37-40

Jesus took no one with Him into the room of the
child except the father and mother, along with
Peter, James and John.

It was the custom of the Jewish people to
mourn the dead for seven days. During this time a
pipe was blown that produced a loud, ear-piercing
shrill tone that mixed with the cries of the mourn-
ers.

When Jesus arrived and announced that the
child was only asleep, the Bible says, "They
laughed Him to scorn." In other words, the religious leaders of the day ridiculed Jesus for making
what they believed was a ludicrous statement. But
it turned out to be totally true!

And he took the damsel by the hand,
and said unto her, Talitha cumi; which is,
being interpreted, Damsel, I say unto thee,
arise. And straightway the damsel arose,
and walked; for she was of the age of

twelve years. And they were astonished with a great astonishment.

—Mark 5:41,42

Think of the glory in Jesus' compassion when He raised Jairus' daughter and returned her to her father's delicate care.

I can only imagine Jesus gazing into this child's eyes after commanding her to come back from the door of death saying, "Little lamb, sit up." With the devotion of a shepherd, He had brought back the one lamb whom the wolves had taken from among the other 99. He ushered her back into the sheepfold.

The glory of the resurrection of Jairus' daughter illuminated his soul. I can almost hear the words of the psalmist ringing in his ears, "Thy word is a lamp unto my feet, and a light unto my path" (Psalms 119:105). Jairus was once again able to live up to the honor of his name, "he awakens."

THE ANOINTING IS AVAILABLE FOR YOU

Maybe you are at the end of yourself. Possibly

you have power and prestige, but your promised child lays at home battling some debilitating disease.

Perhaps you have spent everything that you have, yet nothing in your life is any better. Maybe you have tried everything else. Maybe you have attempted even the most costly experimental procedures to fight sickness and nothing has worked. However, now faith is building on the inside of you. Hope is being painted, like a fresh anointing, to believe the unbelievable and receive the unimaginable.

The anointing is available to cleanse you, heal you and set you free. However, if your faith still needs strengthened, read on. Your miracle is surely on the way!

Chapter Five

THE DESPERATE FATHER

And ofttimes it hath cast him into the
fire, and into the waters, to destroy him:
but if thou canst do any thing, have compassion on us, and help us. Jesus said unto
him, If thou canst believe, all things are
possible to him that believeth.

—Mark 9:22,23

All throughout the news we are hearing that
America is going back to church. After the terrorist
attacks of Sept. 11, 2001, churches across the country achieved a surge in attendance that has only
recently subsided.

I am thankful and happy that America is return-
ing to the faith of our founding fathers. However, I
am a little concerned about what they are going to
receive when they get there. Will they get the rig-
ors of religion? Will they receive the creeds of cre-

ation? Will they hear the doctrines of men?

My hope and prayer is that the people who return to church, for whatever reason, will instead see a display that outstrips human ability and gives hope beyond the scope of human limitation. I pray they will witness a power—the anointing—which will put them in contact with the reality of a resurrected Christ who broke the bands of wickedness and slew death itself and resurrected from the dead. This is the same anointing which gives power to as many as will call upon His name.

Unfortunately, America and the world are held hostage! Their captors are not a terrorist organization or a political dictator. Rather, it is the deceptive devices of the alien armies of the Antichrist that assail the minds of unsuspecting believers.

Believers and sinners alike pose such questions as, "Can God still heal and deliver?" To which I cannot say anything but, "Absolutely! Stick around and see for yourself!"

IF IT BE THY WILL

Throughout the Bible there are only three major

questions concerning the healing and delivering anointing of Jesus Christ, the Anointed One. The first asks the question, "If it be thy will."

> And there came a leper to him, beseeching him, and kneeling down to him, and saying unto him, If thou wilt, thou canst make me clean. And Jesus, moved with compassion, put forth his hand, and touched him, and saith unto him, ~~I will,~~ be thou clean. And as soon as he had spoken, immediately the leprosy departed from him, and he was cleansed.
>
> —Mark 1:40-42

If it were really God's will to heal and deliver one person and not the other, I believe that there would be at least one instance like this in the Bible. However, God's response to this leper was a resounding, "I will!"

I don't know what you have been told, but I know this: healing and deliverance are not mere promises. They are facts. Therefore, if God didn't want to heal or deliver you, He shouldn't have.

The Bible says,

Surely he hath borne our griefs, and carried our sorrows: yet we did esteem him stricken, smitten of God, and afflicted. But he was wounded for our transgressions, he was bruised for our iniquities: the chastisement of our peace was upon him; and with his stripes we are healed.

—Isaiah 53:4,5

WILL YOU BE HEALED?

The second question concerning your healing and deliverance is, "Will you be made whole?"

The Gospel of John records the story of the man by the pool of Bethesda.

Now there is at Jerusalem by the sheep market a pool, which is called in the Hebrew tongue Bethesda, having five porches. In these lay a great multitude of impotent folk, of blind, halt, withered, waiting for the moving of the water. For an angel went down at a certain season into the pool, and troubled the water: whosoever then first after the troubling of the water stepped in was made whole of whatsoever disease he had. And a certain man was there, which had an infirmity thirty and eight years. When Jesus saw him lie, and knew that he had been now a long time in that case, he saith unto him, Wilt thou be made whole? The impotent man answered him, Sir, I have no man, when the water is troubled, to put me into the pool: but while I am coming, another steppeth down before me. Jesus saith unto him, Rise, take up thy bed, and walk. And immediately the man was made whole, and took up his bed, and walked: and on the same day was the sabbath.

—John 5:2-9

Will you be made whole? Are you tired of the struggle, the pain, the bondage, the infirmity, the darkness, the loneliness, the insecurity and the confusion! It's time to reach out and touch the Lord!

Where there is doubt concerning the will of God, faith is strangled and dies. Why? Because faith begins where the will of God is known.

What is the will of God? Third John 1:2 says, "Beloved, I wish above all things that thou mayest prosper and be in health, even as thy soul prospereth."

Jesus removed all doubt by performing an indisputable act of authority—by commanding the man to take up his bed and walk.

If Thou Canst

The last question asked to Jesus regarding healing and deliverance is, "If thou can heal. . ." This is the question I want to focus on because the story is so dramatic.

A father had a boy that cast himself into the fire, thrashing, gnawing like a wild man. He came to Jesus and said, "Master, I took my son to your disciples, and they could not heal him."

I believe this father wanted to take his son to Jesus. But because Jesus was not in the vicinity he brought him to His disciples instead. The result was fruitless—they could not deliver the child.

There is a nursery rhyme that goes, "Humpty Dumpty sat on a wall. Humpty Dumpty had a great fall. All the king's horses and all the king's men couldn't put Humpty Dumpty back together again." My question is, why do we busy ourselves with the king's horses and the king's men? We need to take our burdens directly to the King!

A deadening blow had struck at the very heart of this father's natural hope. I believe the failure of the disciples to heal the child was to show that all hope should be directed to Jesus Christ only. There is an old hymn which says, "My hope is built on nothing less than Jesus' blood and righteousness. I dare not trust the sweetest frame but wholly lean on Jesus name."

You need to trust nothing less than Jesus for your anointing!

Bring the Boy to Me

I love what happens next in this account:

> And one of the multitude answered and said, Master, I have brought unto thee my son, which hath a dumb spirit; And wheresoever he taketh him, he teareth him:

and he foameth, and gnasheth with his teeth, and pineth away: and I spake to thy disciples that they should cast him out; and they could not. He answereth him, and saith, O faithless generation, how long shall I be with you? how long shall I suffer you? bring him unto me.

—Mark 9:17-19

The desperate father did as Jesus asked:

And they brought him unto him: and when he saw him, straightway the spirit tare him; and he fell on the ground, and wallowed foaming. And he asked his father, How long is it ago since this came unto him? And he said, Of a child. And oft-times it hath cast him into the fire, and into the waters, to destroy him: but if thou canst do any thing, have compassion on us, and help us.

—Mark 9:20-22

Jesus, with blazing eyes, locked into the face of that father and declared, "Don't question what I can do. For it is not a question what I can do, but only what you can believe. For all things are possible to him that believes."

The Bible goes on to say,

> And straightway the father of the child cried out, and said with tears, Lord, I believe; help thou mine unbelief. When Jesus saw that the people came running together, he rebuked the foul spirit, saying unto him, Thou dumb and deaf spirit, I charge thee, come out of him, and enter no more into him. And the spirit cried, and rent him sore, and came out of him: and he was as one dead; insomuch that many said, He is dead. But Jesus took him by the hand, and lifted him up; and he arose.
>
> —Mark 9:24-27

Jesus allowed this desperate father to give the prognosis of his child's condition. I believe he wanted the crowd who had gathered to witness the type of miracle that was about to take place.

We need to ask the Lord specifically for what

we want. James 4:3 declares, "Ye ask, and receive not, because ye ask amiss, that ye may consume it upon your lusts."

Right in the middle of this father's dissertation, the boy began to have an uncontrollable fit. At that moment, this father had a choice. He could discard his faith and give up, or direct his faith and be lifted up.

The desperateness of this father gives keen insight into the greatness of God's mercy for us. Even in the midst of doubting, because he had been through everything, there was faith as the grain of mustard seed to believe for anything. This man needed a breakthrough. He needed a sudden burst of the advanced knowledge, or revelation, of God, to push him through his surrounding circumstances.

Like the desperate father of the possessed boy, there is a time designated by God when His anointing will push you through.

THE ANOINTED ONE

This desperate father needed to know this man

called Jesus of Nazareth, the Anointed One. He and his son needed to be touched by the anointing. He needed to know the Christ described in Luke 4.

It was into this setting that Jesus walked and was baptized:

> And John bare record, saying, I saw the Spirit descending from heaven like a dove, and it abode upon him. And I knew him not: but he that sent me to baptize with water, the same said unto me, Upon whom thou shalt see the Spirit descending, and remaining on him, the same is he which baptizeth with the Holy Ghost.
>
> —John 1:32,33

Just after this solitary event between Father and Son, this seemingly common man spent forty days in the wilderness. There He was tempted, tried and tested in every possible way a mere mortal could be. He was tempted in His body as Satan beckoned Him to turn a stone to bread.

Our Lord was tormented in His mind as the Seducer promised Him this world's power and possessions. Jesus was enticed in His spirit to doubt

His heavenly Father's own word. But each time He overcame with the words, "It is written."

Now He was ready for His inauguration into His earthly ministry and the anointing He was destined to display. He was prepared to confront the religious order of this day.

> And he taught in their synagogues, being glorified of all. And he came to Nazareth, where he had been brought up: and, as his custom was, he went into the synagogue on the sabbath day, and stood up for to read. And there was delivered unto him the book of the prophet Esaias. And when he had opened the book, he found the place where it was written, The Spirit of the Lord is upon me, because he hath anointed me to preach the gospel to the poor; he hath sent me to heal the brokenhearted, to preach deliverance to the captives, and recovering of sight to the blind, to set at liberty them that are bruised, To preach the acceptable year of the Lord. And he closed the book, and he gave it again to the minister, and sat down. And

the eyes of all them that were in the synagogue were fastened on him. And he began to say unto them, This day is this scripture fulfilled in your ears. And all bare him witness, and wondered at the gracious words which proceeded out of his mouth. And they said, Is not this Joseph's son?
—Luke 4:15-22

Jesus had grown up in Nazareth, and He was known by all of the townspeople. He was one of them. The Son of a carpenter and, no doubt, expected by them and His family to make His living as a carpenter as well. Carpentry is a noble profession. But something had happened to this young man. He was marked from the foundation of the world for another purpose.

At the age of 33 this young Jewish man met up with His cousin, John, who baptized people and preached a paralyzing message, "Repent, for the kingdom of God is at hand!" It was obvious that he possessed some inside information given by divine impartation to prophets.

They said, "Who does He think He is?" I think it's very evident who He thought He was. He knew

He was the one of whom Isaiah prophesied, "And there shall come forth a rod out of the stem of Jesse, and a Branch shall grow out of his roots: And the spirit of the Lord shall rest upon him, the spirit of wisdom and understanding, the spirit of counsel and might, the spirit of knowledge and of the fear of the Lord" (Isaiah 11:1,2).

In every Jewish synagogue there was a seat. No one ever sat there, however, for it was reserved for the Messiah. This was why the religious leaders of Jesus day became so indignant as to try to throw Him off the brow of a hill. In essence they said, "Who does He think He is?"

Jesus knew exactly who He was. He knew He was God Who ascended from the sapphire sill of heaven's glory and invaded humanity in the flesh!

WHO DO MEN SAY I AM?

During the early days of Jesus earthly ministry He questioned Simon Peter as to who men thought He was.

And they said, Some say that thou art John the Baptist: some, Elias; and others, Jeremias, or one of the prophets. He saith unto them, But whom say ye that I am? And Simon Peter answered and said, Thou art the Christ, the Son of the living God.

—Matthew 16:14-16

The Christ, being translated, simply means "the Anointed One who destroys every yoke."

That was what Jesus was hoping to hear:

And Jesus answered and said unto him, Blessed art thou, Simon Barjona: for flesh and blood hath not revealed it unto thee, but my Father which is in heaven. And I say also unto thee, That thou art Peter, and upon this rock I will build my church; and the gates of hell shall not prevail against it.

—Matthew 16:17,18

Whatever has tried to keep you from the blessing He promised, the gates of hell shall not prevail against. In other words, I'm going to give you a revelation that breaks you through every obstacle of Satan has erected.

That is what the desperate father needed more than anything else. He did not only need hope for his son who cast himself into the fire. He needed a revelation of who Jesus was!

AUTHORITY AND ANOINTING PRODUCE MIRACLES

The Gospel of John records,

> For as the Father hath life in himself; so hath he given to the Son to have life in himself; And hath given him authority to execute judgment also, because he is the Son of man.
>
> —John 5:26,27

Because we were born into the earth, we are "sons of men." One translation says He has given Him authority for and against to execute judgment. Let me say it another way: God has given Jesus authority for us and against the devil to execute judgment. We have the promise of the word of God that God will judge for you and against the devil.

Because you are "a son of man," God has given Jesus power for you and against the devil because He is the Son of man. He hasn't done this because Jesus is the Son of God. Jesus, in the power and authority of the Holy Spirit, performed the miraculous among men not as God, which would not have been miraculous at all, but as a Spirit-anointed man.

The authority in the earth realm comes to you because you have an earth suit—a body. Obviously, to exaggerate the point, you are unable to accomplish anything on the earth without a body!

Jesus said, "God is a Spirit: and they that worship him must worship him in spirit and in truth" (John 4:24).

Herein lies one of the answers to one of the greatest questions that has plagued the mind of man. If God is a loving God, why are babies being aborted? Why are people starving to death? Why are wars and rumors of wars all over the face of the earth? Why is there drug addiction? Why are the hospital beds full? Why do deadly diseases like cancer and AIDS ravage our population?

Genesis 1:26 says, "And God said, Let us make man in our image, after our likeness: and let them have dominion over the fish of the sea, and over the fowl of the air, and over the cattle, and over all the earth, and over every creeping thing that creepeth upon the earth." God gave us dominion in all the earth.

John 10:1 says, "Verily, verily, I say unto you, He that entereth not by the door into the sheepfold, but climbeth up some other way, the same is a thief and a robber."

Jesus said of Himself, "Verily, verily, I say unto you, I am the door of the sheep" (John 10:7).

What was Jesus talking about? He was referring to the devil, the thief. That thief came to steal, kill and destroy. That thief, the devil, came in to the earth another way. The devil gained entry into this earth illegally! He is a reprobate! He is a loser! He's an intruder! He is here illegally all because he has no body.

God, being a Spirit, cannot do anything without a body. This is the reason He said,

> For the eyes of the Lord run to and fro throughout the whole earth, to shew himself strong in the behalf of them whose heart is perfect toward him. Herein thou

hast done foolishly: therefore from hence-
forth thou shalt have wars.

—2 Chronicles 16:9

That's why Jesus said be filled with the Spirit.
Why didn't He say for the Spirit to get filled with
you? Because a Spirit has no authority in this earth.
The authority of having an earth suit gives you the
opportunity to manifest miracles, but the anointing
gives you the ability to manifest miracles.

DELIVERANCE HAS COME

I want to share with you a modern-day miracle
of a desperate father and mother who reached out
in faith to Jesus.

Not long ago pastor and his wife sent in a T-
shirt to Dominion Camp Meeting believing God to
deliver their son from drug addiction. When the T-
shirt was returned, the mother ironed it and laid it
on her son's bed, believing her son would come
back home.

Two months later Matthew came home and put
the T-shirt on. He went out that night to buy some

Methamphetamines to shoot into his arms. But the drug house he usually hung out in had shut down, and all the dealers he knew refused to sell to him, saying their relationship was over. Two months later Matthew surrendered his life to Jesus.

On Wednesday night of the Raise the Standard Pastors' and Church Workers' Conference, Matthew and his dad were ordained into the World Harvest Church Ministerial Fellowship.

It was a tremendous night for this pastor because Matthew grew up in institutions, never walked across a platform and never finished high school. To walk across that platform with his son who now serves in their church was such an honor. Matthew oversees the praise & worship and the youth ministry for his father. They are expecting to revolutionize their city.

It was to a world such as ours to which Jesus came. If there were any less need for Him, He would not have come. Just like the desperate father needed to take desperate measures to see his son delivered, so you must refuse to allow anything to stand in the way of your miracle.

Like the desperate father questioned, "If thou canst, help us." Jesus looks at you and says, "If you can believe, all things are possible."

Jesus Christ has discounted every excuse you could offer to stay sick and oppressed. He limited Himself to the same power available to you today—the anointing of the Holy Spirit.

The apostle Peter told Cornelius,

> The word which God sent unto the children of Israel, preaching peace by Jesus Christ: (he is Lord of all:) That word, I say, ye know, which was published throughout all Judaea, and began from Galilee, after the baptism which John preached; How God anointed Jesus of Nazareth with the Holy Ghost and with power: who went about doing good, and healing all that were oppressed of the devil; for God was with him. And we are witnesses of all things which he did both in the land of the Jews, and in Jerusalem; whom they slew and hanged on a tree: Him God raised up the third day, and shewed him openly; Not to all the people, but unto witnesses chosen before of God, even to us, who did eat and drink with him after he

rose from the dead.

—Acts 10:36-41

In the next chapter, I will show you from the word of God how you possess the powerful anointing of the Holy Spirit to perform indisputable acts of authority.

Chapter Six

THE BROKEN MULTITUDES

Several years ago, a little girl in our congregation was dying from an incurable disease. Her parents shared with my wife, Joni, and said, "We have one of her bed sheets with us, and we would like Pastor Parsley to pray over it. After he does we are going to put it on the bed and let her sleep on it."

Joni shared this with me during the service. I wrapped the bed sheet around my shoulders, and I preached the entire service that way. I gave the sheet back to that mother and she placed it on her daughter's bed. Within a week that little girl was completely healed—not because of Rod Parsley, but because of the healing power of almighty God!

A power just like this family experienced is available to you. It is beyond anything you could ever comprehend. This power goes beyond any-thing that any electric company knows anything about. This force is greater than the political machines in operation on this planet. Its impact goes beyond what a doctor can do for you. It will drive you to lift your hands in the valley of your life when everything around you is crumbling.

This supernatural propulsion offers hope when you don't have a dollar to change. It extends hope when the doctors look at you and say you have to die and cannot live. It brings hope in the midst of hopeless situations.

You can walk in the very anointing of God!

THE TANGIBLE ANOINTING

I remember times when Dr. Lester Sumrall was alive and we would be sitting together in a service. Sometimes he would reach over and pat me on the knee. I would say to myself, "Yes, Lord, I want the anointing that is upon His life."

I'm in covenant with Dr. Sumrall, because I'm still in submission to the authority of what he spoke while he was on this earth. I still do not do the things that he taught me not to do. I still do the things that he taught me to do.

He taught me to clean out a sink after using the washroom in somebody else's home. But he also taught me how to cast the devil out of a demon-oppressed individual. He taught me and trained me because I heard him.

Dr. Lester Sumrall is in my spiritual genealogy. He had authority because he was a man under authority. He could call, and things would happen. I saw him a thousand times put those hands, three fingers on a forehead, take a breath, and wait on the Holy Ghost and then say, "Come out!" and witness demons flee.

I saw him set 2,000 demonically oppressed people free in one fifteen-second prayer. He cast the devil out of one girl in a prison, and 150,000 people were saved, and the newspaper headlines read, "The Devil is Dead." That's who I'm talking about.

Behind Dr. Sumrall, in his spiritual lineage—the great two-fisted plumber, Smith Wigglesworth, who grabbed a man that had been dead for three days out of a casket, stuck him up against the wall as a corpse, commanded that he live, and he coughed and walked out of the funeral parlor with all of his family and friends standing there watching.

This man read the Bible incessantly thirty minutes every morning, and then prayed thirty minutes, then read thirty minutes, then prayed thirty minutes, read thirty minutes, then prayed thirty minutes. That's the way he lived.

Brother Sumrall showed up one day to bring a newspaper into his house.

"What's that in your hand," Wigglesworth said.

Brother Sumrall said, "Well, it's the newspaper, sir."

Wigglesworth replied, "Leave that outside my house. There's only one kind of news inside these doors, and that's the Gospel."

My spiritual genealogy includes the great Howard Carter, who brought the revelation of all nine gifts of the Spirit to the body of Christ, the greatest revelation given since the day of Pentecost. Every major Pentecostal denomination of the world uses his writings as the bedrock of all revelation concerning the nine gifts of the Spirit in 1 Corinthians.

And behind those men, there are others. And

there are many more whose names I could call, but it would do no good, because you don't know them.

I have, in my spiritual genealogy, the great Kenneth Copeland, who spends hours on end on the phone with me, pouring his life into me. The late John Osteen often sat me at his feet and instructed me in the things of God, and there was an impartation that took place.

But here's the good news. When I speak, we're all speaking the same thing. Who? Everybody that is in that spiritual genealogy. That's the reason the Bible says in Hebrews 12:1,2, "Wherefore seeing we also are compassed about with so great a cloud of witnesses, let us lay aside every weight, and the sin which doth so easily beset us, and let us run with patience the race that is set before us, Looking unto Jesus the author and finisher of our faith; who for the joy that was set before him endured the cross, despising the shame, and is set down at the right hand of the throne of God."

We are compassed around about with so great a cloud of witnesses, the spirits of just men made perfect, already completed their perfection. Therefore, when I speak into your life, you receive an impartation that's been passed down to me. In other words, you are going to get a touch of the faith I received from Dr. Sumrall when he passed the sword to me.

How did Dr. Sumrall get such faith? Because in their last meeting in London, England, Smith Wigglesworth wrapped his arms around Lester Sumrall and began to pray, and his prayer was simply this. "Let the faith that is in my heart come into this young man." Wigglesworth cried so much that the top of Brother Sumrall's head was wet with his tears. They never saw each other again – not on this planet, at least!

In this final hour, this same impartation can come in you through God's tangible transfer! We will all speak the same thing, and it's going to come through an impartation.

You will get something you didn't bargain for. And, if you trace the thing all the way back, it goes back through Elijah and Samuel, Elisha, Daniel, Nahum, Habakkuk, Moses, Daniel, David, Peter and Paul just to name a few.

When you begin to get this revelation, you can stand and begin to call, and God will answer you.

The next time you're in the middle of your winter, and you start to speak to the fevered brow of your infant child, and there's nobody there, remember, everybody's there. The tangible transfer of God's miracle anointing is present with you!

There is an anointing sufficient enough to break every chain and to destroy every yoke. I shared with you at the beginning of the book that the anointing is not only tangible, but it is also transferable.

What does that mean? Let's look at Pentecostal Headquarters, the Book of Acts. Luke the physician records,

> And believers were the more added to the Lord, multitudes both of men and women. Insomuch that they brought forth the sick into the streets, and laid them on beds and couches, that at the least the shadow of Peter passing by might overshadow some of them.
>
> —Acts 5:14,15

After Jesus' resurrection and the infilling of the Holy Spirit on the day of Pentecost, the church grew dramatically. During one revival service, 5,000 men alone were saved. But great impartation never comes without great persecution.

On several occasions the disciples were beaten and commanded not to speak in the name of Jesus. But still, souls were added to the church daily.

Signs and wonders were so prevalent that many would bring family and friends who were sick, lame, halt, blind, deaf and dumb and lay them in the streets. They watched the way Peter went to temple every day. They knew what time he went and what route he walked, and they said, "If perchance the shadow of Peter might be cast over us we may be healed."

What caused such a fascination? It didn't have anything to do with Peter's shadow! The attraction of such a host of people was because of something commonly known as the anointing. When Peter, full of the Holy Ghost, would begin to walk down the street, his shadow would touch those that were lame, blind, deaf and dumb. And miraculously, people would walk, see, hear and speak again.

This anointing was also tangible upon the clothing of the apostle Paul.

And God wrought special miracles by the hands of Paul: So that from his body were brought unto the sick handkerchiefs or aprons, and the diseases departed from them, and the evil spirits went out of them.

—Acts 19:11,12

I want to begin to see the church walk in the manifested tangible presence of God. Some say those days are over. But I believe the book of Acts will seem like a Sunday school picnic compared to what is going to happen during our lifetime!

THE YOKE-DESTROYING, BURDEN-REMOVING ANOINTING

One of the greatest characteristics of the end-time body of Christ is that it will operate in the spontaneous move of the Holy Spirit because of the anointing upon the lives of believers. The day of personality and persona will be over! The time of masquerading pulpiteers will be no more!

As a Christian, you are not working up to something. You are already in something. You are in the divine flow of almighty God. Isaiah 10:27 says, "And it shall come to pass in that day, that his burden shall be taken away from off thy shoulder, and his yoke from off thy neck, and the yoke shall be destroyed because of the anointing."

It's the anointing that destroys the yoke! This verse didn't say that the anointing would break the yoke. It said the anointing would destroy the yoke upon your life. There is a difference between break and destroy. If you break something, it is possible that it will come back because someone can fix it.

The actual Hebrew translation of the word translated "destroyed" is "to cause to cease to be as if it never existed." I like to refer to it as annihilation. Through the anointing the forces of light will bombard the forces of darkness that are arrayed against you!

I am not referring to some man-made power! I am not referring to something that will just barely get you by! I am not referring to something that will get you free for a few days and then your bondage comes back! I am referring to something that will destroy the yoke of bondage off of your life! The anointing is the reason the apostle Paul could tell the churches at Rome, "Nay, in all these things we are more than conquerors through him that loved us" (Romans 8:37).

First John 3:8 declares, "He that committeth sin is of the devil; for the devil sinneth from the beginning. For this purpose the Son of God was manifested, that he might destroy the works of the devil." If Jesus was sent to destroy, or annihilate, the works of the devil, then they are annihilated in your life.

The prison door is open. But my question to you is, what are you still doing inside when He made a way out? You and I are serving a God that is a way maker!

WHO IS THE LORD?

Let's look again at Isaiah 10:27 at the word "yoke"—which means the oppression. The word "oppress" means "to rule over you."

Whenever sickness, disease or bondage have their tentacles wrapped around your life, they are lording or ruling over you. It is time for anything that is trying to gain authority over you, to recognize who alone has the rightful claim to that authority.

Pharaoh, when addressing Moses about the

deliverance of the children of Israel from Egyptian bondage, asked, "Who is the Lord, that I should obey his voice to let Israel go? I know not the Lord, neither will I let Israel go" (Exodus 5:2).

It is time for the spirit of infirmity to find out who is Lord. It's time for the spirit of depression to find out who's really Lord. It's time for the spirit of discouragement to discover who the Lord is!

The apostle John wrote, "Little children, keep yourselves from idols" (1 John 5:21). An idol is anything to which lordship is directed in your life. Lordship is anything that has authority over you. If there's anything right now that has authority over you, it is my prayer that before you finish this book, a river of living water will swell up on the inside of you and that yoke of oppression will be destroyed because of the anointing. It actually says the yoke shall be destroyed in the presence of the anointing.

Let me share with you another testimony of the tangible anointing of the Lord destroying oppression in someone's life.

Grenada knew the Lord at one time, but had returned to a life of crack and prostitution. Then she started watching *Breakthrough* and requested a prayer cloth. She awoke on a Monday morning alone, burned out on drugs, out of money, out of food and facing eviction. As she laid in her bed in total despair, tired and ready to die, she heard the mailman. Her prayer cloth had arrived!

She stumbled back to bed, putting the cloth on her head. As she pulled the covers over her head she cried, "God, just let me die." Within minutes she was in the bathroom vomiting. She was instantaneously delivered that morning. That same week she received a one hundred-fold return on her seed sown into *Breakthrough*, which was more than enough to pay her bills!

Today, Grenada is back in church, running "The House That Love Built" and ministering to women with situations similar to hers.

Don't ever doubt it: the anointing is tangible. It doesn't matter if it's Moses' face, Elijah's mantle, Elisha's bones, Peter's shadow or Paul's handkerchiefs and aprons. When Grenada came in contact with that anointing on that prayer cloth, five minutes later she was saved, delivered and glorifying God!

THE FRAGRANCE OF THE ANOINTING

In the Levitical priesthood, there was a ritual of preparing a special holy oil. Poignant herbs were pressed into the oil, making it aromatic. According to law, this mixture was unique to the priesthood. When a priest was set apart and anointed, the oil represented a type of the New Testament anointing of the Holy Spirit.

The scent of the anointing oil was distinctive. If someone was near an Old Testament priest, he could literally smell the anointing upon him. Such an anointing could not be kept a secret.

When the early church was anointed, it was apparent. The book of Acts records several instances of our spiritual forefathers being filled with the Holy Spirit.

Today, God is still the same. James 1:17 still states, "Every good gift and every perfect gift is from above, and cometh down from the Father of lights, with whom is no variableness, neither shadow of turning." His power and authority through the Holy Spirit have not changed. He is still anointing men and women today.

You can receive the anointing of the Holy

Spirit, but you can't hide this phenomenon that it works upon your life. Its sweet savor will attract people and blessing to your life.

ALL THINGS ARE POSSIBLE

The anointing of God is a tangible thing. It has substance. Its substance is energy. As I stated earlier, the anointing is a perpetual propulsion of the power of God which will drive you through a line of Satan's defense.

You have an anointing. You have an unction from God. You have within your being perpetual propulsion of power from on high. It may need stirred up, but it's in you.

There is the wonderful story of a little girl born in southern California. The joys and the ecstasy of parenthood turned into the horrors of a nightmare as that little baby girl, named Betty, came out of the womb. Her body and limbs were disfigured almost beyond recognition. For fourteen long years that little girl lay upon a bed, a hopeless invalid.

Her mother didn't know a lot about the Bible, but she found a verse of scripture and made it her own. It said, "With men it is impossible, but not with God: for with God all things are possible" (Mark 10:27).

For fourteen years Betty never wore a piece of clothing. It would not cover her twisted limbs. For fourteen years Betty had never had a bite of food cross her tongue. She was fed with a tube into her stomach and intravenously. She had all of her mental faculties and was a bright girl, but day after day she lay at home, never getting any better.

One day her mother came in and said, "Betty, I don't know how you're going to take this, but I was reading the Bible the other day."

Betty interrupted, "Wait a minute, Mama. I had a dream, and in the dream God spoke to me and said, 'All things were possible to him that believeth.'"

Betty's mother said, "That's the verse that God gave me." Then she went ran and told her pastor.

Her pastor said, "Well, we don't want to get our hopes up." Why not? Most people have more hope in an aspirin than they do in eternal God.

Betty's mother retorted, "God promised my little girl and me that on Sunday afternoon, Jesus is going to heal her body."

So on Sunday afternoon, everyone showed up to see what God was not going to do. They were standing outside looking through the windows. It was documented in all the newspapers. Betty said, "Mama, I've never worn a dress or had shoes on my feet. Mama, please buy me a dress and shoes. Then, Mama, hang them on the wall where I can see them, because I am going to wear those clothes on Sunday."

On Sunday, a little white cloud appeared in the living room of their home. It moved down the hallway, into Betty's room, and stopped at the end of her bed. She reached out with a little crooked limb and tried to touch it. However, it was just out of reach.

Afterwards her testimony was that God spoke to her in that moment and said, "Always remember, this has nothing to do with Betty and everything to do with Me."

There comes a time when you can't get your miracle on your own. Try as you will, the heavens seem like brass, and you can't break through.

That little cloud moved over and touched her body. Witnesses said that they thought her body was coming apart, as her joints began to crack. On that fateful afternoon, every bone in her body was straight.

Betty was completed healed. She put on her dress and shoes. Then she walked around her house with her arms raised in praise to God saying, "All things are possible to him that believeth."

Today Betty is alive and well preaching the Gospel of Jesus Christ. I want you to know the anointing of God is a tangible energy, and it will destroy every yoke in your life!

You have something on the inside of you that pushes back the darkness. You have something on the inside of you that dispels the adversary. You have got something bigger than the world on the inside of you. First John 4:4 says, "Ye are of God, little children, and have overcome them: because greater is he that is in you, than he that is in the world."

It doesn't matter what may be coming against you. It is the anointing that breaks every yoke.

If you are a born-again believer, the same Jesus that walked the cobblestone streets of Jerusalem, and His anointing, now dwell inside of you. The Bible says, "To whom God would make known what is the riches of the glory of this mystery among the Gentiles; which is Christ in you, the hope of glory" (Colossians 1:27).

In another place the anointing is referred to as, "But we have this treasure in earthen vessels, that the excellency of the power may be of God, and not of us" (2 Corinthians 4:7).

There's something called the anointing of the Holy Ghost living inside of you. There's something within you that is bigger than you. It is not only bigger than you—it is bigger than all your problems. It is bigger than all your fears. It is bigger than any mountain you can or cannot see.

John 7:38 says, "He that believeth on me, as the scripture hath said, out of his belly shall flow rivers of living water."

Your spirit becomes the generator that takes the Word of God and changes it into the fuel that the Holy Ghost uses to produce the anointing in your life.

GREATER WORKS

If you have the anointing of the Holy Spirit and His presence in your life, you should be able to do what Jesus did during earthly ministry. The Bible says so.

Jesus proclaimed,

> Verily, verily, I say unto you, He that believeth on me, the works that I do shall he do also; and greater works than these shall he do; because I go unto my Father. And whatsoever ye shall ask in my name, that will I do, that the Father may be glorified in the Son.
>
> —John 14:12,13

Jesus performed miracles for just a few short years in Jerusalem and the surrounding towns. But His disciples and the unending generations after them performed, and continue to perform, miracles all around the world through the anointing of the Holy Spirit.

You are anointed, and if the Lord ever has His hand on you, He has it on you now! You have an anointing, and that anointing can destroy every yoke!

Your prayer should be, "Lord, give me oil and give me wine."

Be glad then, ye children of Zion, and rejoice in the Lord your God: for he hath given you the former rain moderately, and he will cause to come down for you the rain, the former rain, and the latter rain in the first month. And the floors shall be full of wheat, and the fats shall overflow with wine and oil.

—Joel 2:23,24

A dying world is desperately looking to the church for a power to deliver them from their sin-sick state. Through the anointing of the Holy Spirit, we have their answer. We have no right to keep it to ourselves. God will help us, for He promised He would work with us to confirm His Word. And, He will do above all that we could ever imagine.

We have this hope that, as the apostle John wrote,

Beloved, now are we the sons of God, and it doth not yet appear what we shall be: but we know that, when he shall appear, we shall be like him; for we shall see him as he is.

—1 John 3:2

The anointing will make a spiritual warrior and protector out of a backslidden father. The anointing will transform the distraught mother into a powerful intercessor. The anointing will change a calloused teenager into a mighty witness for God. The anointing will transfigure a beaten-down preacher into a blazing prophet!

The last recorded Gospel in the Bible declares,

> And there are also many other things which Jesus did, the which, if they should be written every one, I suppose that even the world itself could not contain the books that should be written. Amen.
>
> —John 21:25

Chapter Seven

WIND AND FIRE

The disciples of Jesus had walked with Him for more than three years. They had watched him exhibit mastery over demons, disease and death. They had seen the blind receive sight, the lame stand upright and walk, lepers leap for joy and their leisions vanished and the dead rise and live again.

Those same disciples fled when Jesus was arrested and taken to stand trial. They skulked in the midst of crowds while He was carried through the streets of Jerusalem and whipped like a dog. They watched helplessly as the Romans soldiers drove nails through His hands and feet. They saw His precious blood drip from His wounds until it stained the wood of the cross and soaked the sands where it was driven into the ground. Finally, they watched Him give up His life.

Their hopes were crushed. All that they had hoped for was gone with their leader's breath. They had left everything behind to follow Jesus, and now He was gone. But on the third day, the brightness of His glory rolled the stone away, and Jesus of Nazareth came forth in resurrected splendor!

WAIT FOR THE PROMISE

Jesus conquered death. The disciples were ready to begin again. Joyfully they gathered around their risen Lord: "When they therefore were come together, they asked of him, saying, Lord, wilt thou at this time restore again the kingdom to Israel?" (Acts 1:6)

In their minds, they were sure He would now break the yoke of Roman oppression and make Israel a powerful nation again. In their hearts, they must have been positive He would set up His earthly kingdom and allow them to rule and reign beside Him in a kingdom of priests.

But Jesus had other ideas:

And, being assembled together with

them, commanded them that they should not depart from Jerusalem, but wait for the promise of the Father, which, saith he, ye have heard of me. For John truly baptized with water; but ye shall be baptized with the Holy Ghost not many days hence.

—Acts 1:4,5

There was work to do and a world to win, but even those who knew Jesus best would not be able to do it in their own strength. Jesus told the disciples,

But ye shall receive power, after that the Holy Ghost is come upon you: and ye shall be witnesses unto me both in Jerusalem, and in all Judaea, and in Samaria, and unto the uttermost part of the earth.

—Acts 1:8

The disciples held a ten-day prayer meeting. They closed themselves in and gave themselves over to praising God and seeking His will. They had a promise of power and devoted themselves to waiting until it came.

The fiftieth day after the resurrection, the Feast of Pentecost, was the day God chose to roll back the heavens and introduce the third person of the Trinity:

> And when the day of Pentecost was fully come, they were all with one accord in one place. And suddenly there came a sound from heaven as of a rushing mighty wind, and it filled all the house where they were sitting. And there appeared unto them cloven tongues like as of fire, and it sat upon each of them. And they were all filled with the Holy Ghost, and began to speak with other tongues, as the Spirit gave them utterance.
>
> —Acts 2:1-4

When the Spirit came upon them, they all began to speak in tongues and the room could not contain the noise of them. A crowd gathered, attracted by the noise and commotion. Some saw their joy and thought they were drunk. Others were confused and asked each other what it all meant.

Many were amazed, because they were hearing the wonderful works of God in their native languages.

The Holy Spirit is what made the disciples different! Their prayer lives change completely. From Pentecost on, whenever they prayed, they were filled with the power of the Spirit.

Their witnessing changed. Peter, who once denied knowing Jesus and cowered before the accusations of a little girl, boldly preached a sermon that led 3,000 people to seek their baptism that very day.

Their priorities changed. They left their fishing boats behind as they went forth to spread the good news, shining in the light of the Gospel. They preached on the steps of the temple, in the village of Samaria and in the cities of Judea. They set off to take the Word of God as far as they could go.

The power released on Pentecost lit a fire that spread the Gospel throughout the whole world. And yet today, through you it is doing the same thing!

SIGNS OF THE SPIRIT

One of the ways God has characterized Himself is with the wind.

When Noah and his family were saved from the flood, they floated in the ark on the surface of the water for 150 days. That must have seemed a long time to spend with a zoo starter kit aboard! There was no dry land anywhere until God provided a wind:

> And God remembered Noah, and every living thing, and all the cattle that was with him in the ark: and God made a wind to pass over the earth, and the waters assuaged; The fountains also of the deep and the windows of heaven were stopped, and the rain from heaven was restrained; And the waters returned from off the earth continually: and after the end of the hundred and fifty days the waters were abated. And the ark rested in the seventh month, on the seventeenth day of the month, upon the mountains of Ararat. And the waters decreased continually until the tenth month: in the tenth month, on the first day of the month, were the tops of the mountains seen.
>
> —Genesis 8:1-5

God's power, manifested in the wind, decreased the waters and provided a dwelling place for those He had preserved.

When Moses led the children of Israel out of bondage, they found themselves trapped between an impending onslaught of Egyptian soldiers and an unyielding sea. Blocked from the Promise land and facing certain death, they cried out to God for help. He responded with a wind:

> And Moses stretched out his hand over the sea; and the Lord caused the sea to go back by a strong east wind all that night, and made the sea dry land, and the waters were divided. And the children of Israel went into the midst of the sea upon the dry ground: and the waters were a wall unto them on their right hand, and on their left. . . And the Lord said unto Moses, Stretch out thine hand over the sea, that the waters may come again upon the Egyptians, upon their chariots, and upon their horsemen. And Moses stretched forth his hand over the sea, and the sea returned to his strength when the morning appeared; and the

Egyptians fled against it; and the Lord overthrew the Egyptians in the midst of the sea. And the waters returned, and covered the chariots, and the horsemen, and all the host of Pharaoh that came into the sea after them; there remained not so much as one of them. But the children of Israel walked upon dry land in the midst of the sea; and the waters were a wall unto them on their right hand, and on their left.

—Exodus 14:21,22, 26-29

On the day of Pentecost, the gathered disciples experienced the sound of a mighty, rushing wind. God's power, manifested in the wind, separated the disciples forever from their former lives of weakness and fear. He filled the disciples with the life-changing power to do, in one decade, what Israel had not been able to do in the entirety of the Old Testament! Propelled by the wind of God, the Gospel spread throughout the world and created the church of Jesus Christ, against which the gates of hell shall not prevail.

God also distinguishes His Spirit by fire. After Adam and Eve rebelled, God used fire to drive them out of the garden:

> And the Lord God said, Behold, the
> man is become as one of us, to know good
> and evil: and now, lest he put forth his
> hand, and take also of the tree of life, and
> eat, and live for ever: Therefore the Lord
> God sent him forth from the garden of
> Eden, to till the ground from whence he
> was taken. So he drove out the man; and he
> placed at the east of the garden of Eden
> Cherubim, and a flaming sword which
> turned every way, to keep the way of the
> tree of life.
>
> —Genesis 3:22-24

Throughout the Old Testament, God has manifested Himself as fire:

- Moses received the call on his life when God spoke to Him in a burning bush.
- God led the children of Israel as a pillar of fire by night.
- Offerings to God were burned on His altar with fire.

- The prophet Elijah challenged the false priests of Baal to a contest to prove the power of God. After they changed and prayed to their false god with no results, "Then the fire of the Lord fell, and consumed the burnt sacrifice, and the wood, and the stones, and the dust, and licked up the water that was in the trench" (1 Kings 18:38).
- The prophet Jeremiah cried out, "I will not make mention of him, nor speak any more in his name. But his word was in mine heart as a burning fire shut up in my bones, and I was weary with forbearing, and I could not stay" (Jeremiah 20:9).

Fire has both a good and destructive nature. It can burn something to oblivion or refine it to permanence. Although fire burns weeds into ashes and destroys infection, it also closes wounds and tempers steel. When the power of the Holy Ghost takes hold of a human heart yielded to God, it spreads like a wildfire!

WIND + FIRE = CHANGE

You are living in the dispensation of the Holy Ghost. This time from the resurrection of Christ until the close of the age is the age of grace—the time appointed by God for the Holy Ghost to reveal Jesus Christ to the world.

Jesus said,

> But when the Comforter is come, whom I will send unto you from the Father, even the Spirit of truth, which proceedeth from the Father, he shall testify of me.
> —John 15:26

The Holy Spirit is even your intercessor before the throne of God! The apostle Paul wrote,

> Likewise the Spirit also helpeth our infirmities: for we know not what we should pray for as we ought: but the Spirit itself maketh intercession for us with groanings which cannot be uttered. And he that searcheth the hearts knoweth what is the mind of the Spirit, because he maketh

intercession for the saints according to the will of God.

—Romans 8:26,27

Only the Holy Spirit can cause true, permanent change in a person's character. He can take hold of the vilest sinner and make him spotlessly clean. Only the Holy Ghost can minister healing to the sorrowing human heart. He can light the gospel fire in their hearts and send them blazing out into a world that needs to know God!

The experience of Pentecost is available today. If you have been born again, you can experience the infilling of the Spirit of God, also known as the baptism in the Holy Ghost.

God will fill you to overflowing with the power and presence of His Spirit. You will begin to experience a new understanding of the Bible and to pray with clearer direction and power. You will also begin to speak in other tongues, a language given directly by God to help you pray, worship and prophesy.

The baptism of the Holy Ghost will change your life. The disciples who received that power at Pentecost were filled with joy and boldness. They acquired the strength and ability to minister the Word of God mightily. From the Upper Room of Acts 2 to this very day, the Holy Ghost has swept around the world, glorifying God and bringing His life-changing power to men and women in all lands. Let it burn brightly in your life as well!

Conclusion

YOU CAN KNOW HOW
THE STORY ENDS

This book is full of wonderful stories from the Bible and from today of healing, deliverance and salvation. However, let me interject: you don't have to be born again to be healed. Jesus will heal you anyway.

How sad it would be, though, to live this life in health, and in ease, only to open your eyes on the other side of eternity. There you would be surrounded by the howls and the cackles in the bowels of the devil's hell, because you did not have the blessed assurance that Jesus Christ was your Savior.

Tens of thousands of people are in churches across the country and around the world that want to be saved, and try to act saved, but, sadly, have no assurance that they are saved.

I travel quite a bit, and in every crusade that I conduct, nearly ninety percent of those in attendance go to church every Sunday. When I give the altar call, however, it is flooded with nearly two-thirds of the entire crowd, who then pray the sinner's prayer. People are so desperate for an assurance of their salvation that they will latch onto an experience just so they can have something to point to! But it doesn't have to be that way. The Lord promises the eternal security of all those who surrender their lives to Him.

Maybe you are bound by drug addiction, alcohol, self-mutilation, suicidal thoughts, eating disorders or depression. Possibly your body or that of a loved one has been afflicted with cancer, a disability, a terminal illness, migraines or incessant pain. Whatever your situation is, God loves you. Jesus said,

> For God so loved the world, that he gave his only begotten Son, that whosoever believeth in him should not perish, but have everlasting life. For God sent not his

Son into the world to condemn the world;
but that the world through him might be
saved.

—John 3:16,17

I'm reminded of the story of a great hymn
writer, William Cowper who wrote the beloved
song, *There Is A Fountain.* Cowper was highly
respected in English literary circles. However,
throughout his life Cowper continued to be plagued
by periodic melancholy. Often during these periods
he even sought to end his life. It is interesting that
some of his most meaningful hymns were written
after these times. Till the end of his days Cowper
could never completely shake off the belief that
God would not turn His back upon him. On his
death bed, however, it is said that his face lit up as
he uttered these last words, "I am not shut out of
heaven after all."

Unlike Cowper, you can rejoice in knowing—
really knowing—that you are on your way to heav-
en. Romans 10:13 simply states, "For whosoever
shall call upon the name of the Lord shall be
saved."

At this moment, the Lord has stopped in the

midst of your everyday life to deliver you from the clutches of the devil. It doesn't matter what you have done. Heaven is full of thieves, sinners, adulterers and even murderers who have plunged beneath the fountain of Jesus' crimson blood to wash all their guilty stains.

What if this was your one day to be set free—not only from sickness and disease, but also from the terminal disease of sin? What if this was the day you've been waiting on for so long to find a way from under the heavy load of hopeless and helplessness?

After reading this book, you may find yourself ready for a life-changing encounter with Christ, the Anointed One, who takes away the sins of the world. If you have any question in your mind whether or not you are ready to meet God in the next fifteen seconds, I want to say a prayer for you. At the end of that prayer you will be as sure for heaven as if you were already there.

Are you ready? Don't think about anyone or anything. Just say to yourself, "Am I ready to meet God in the pavilions of glory?" If you answered "no" or "I don't know" pray this prayer:

Heavenly Father, I come to you just as I am. I was born a sinner, and I have committed sins. I ask you to forgive me, wash me in your blood, and give me eternal life.

Satan, you're a liar! I renounce you for you are not my god. Get out of my life! Lord Jesus Christ, I accept you, believe in you and confess you as my Savior. I will live for you as you show me how. Now let me know I'm on my way to heaven, and I will praise you the rest of my life.

This is the kind of Jesus you now serve. He will push His way through every barrier, every bondage and ever broken heart just to get to you.

The Gospel of John says,

But as many as received him, to them gave he power to become the sons of God, even to them that believe on his name: Which were born, not of blood, nor of the will of the flesh, nor of the will of man, but of God.

—John 1:12,13

If you prayed this prayer, you are on your way to heaven, and through Jesus Christ's anointing, you are ready to stand against all the powers of Satan! Welcome to the family of God!

ANOINTING SCRIPTURES

And Samuel said unto Jesse, Are here all thy children? And he said, There remaineth yet the youngest, and, behold, he keepeth the sheep. And Samuel said unto Jesse, Send and fetch him: for we will not sit down till he come hither. And he sent, and brought him in. Now he was ruddy, and withal of a beautiful countenance, and goodly to look to. And the Lord said, Arise, anoint him: for this is he. Then Samuel took the horn of oil, and anointed him in the midst of his brethren: and the Spirit of the Lord came upon David from that day forward. So Samuel rose up, and went to Ramah.

—1 Samuel 16:11-13

Touch not mine anointed, and do my prophets no harm.

—1 Chronicles 16:22

Now know I that the Lord saveth his anointed; he will hear him from his holy heaven with the saving strength of his right hand.

—Psalm 20:6

The Lord is my strength and my shield; my heart trusted in him, and I am helped: therefore my heart greatly rejoiceth; and with my song will I praise him. The Lord is their strength, and he is the saving strength of his anointed.

—Psalm 28:7,8

Thou lovest righteousness, and hatest wickedness: therefore God, thy God, hath anointed thee with the oil of gladness above thy fellows.

—Psalm 45:7

There is a river, the streams whereof

shall make glad the city of God, the holy place of the tabernacles of the most High.

—Psalm 46:4

Behold, O God our shield, and look upon the face of thine anointed.

—Psalm 84:9

But my horn shalt thou exalt like the horn of an unicorn: I shall be anointed with fresh oil.

—Psalm 92:10

Behold, I and the children whom the Lord hath given me are for signs and for wonders in Israel from the Lord of hosts, which dwelleth in mount Zion.

—Isaiah 8:18

And it shall come to pass in that day, that his burden shall be taken away from off thy shoulder, and his yoke from off thy neck, and the yoke shall be destroyed because of the anointing.

—Isaiah 10:27

Who hath believed our report? and to whom is the arm of the Lord revealed?

—Isaiah 53:1

Yea, the Lord will answer and say unto his people, Behold, I will send you corn, and wine, and oil, and ye shall be satisfied therewith: and I will no more make you a reproach among the heathen.

—Joel 2:19

And when they had passed over, they came into the land of Gennesaret, and drew to the shore. And when they were come out of the ship, straightway they knew him, And ran through that whole region round about, and began to carry about in beds those that were sick, where they heard he was. And whithersoever he entered, into villages, or cities, or country, they laid the sick in the streets, and besought him that they might touch if it were but the border of his garment: and as many as touched him were made whole.

—Mark 6:53-56

Be glad then, ye children of Zion, and rejoice in the Lord your God: for he hath given you the former rain moderately, and he will cause to come down for you the rain, the former rain, and the latter rain in the first month. And the floors shall be full of wheat, and the fats shall overflow with wine and oil. And I will restore to you the years that the locust hath eaten, the cankerworm, and the caterpiller, and the palmerworm, my great army which I sent among you. And ye shall eat in plenty, and be satisfied, and praise the name of the Lord your God, that hath dealt wondrously with you: and my people shall never be ashamed.

—Joel 2:23-26

And he said unto them, Go ye into all the world, and preach the gospel to every creature. He that believeth and is baptized shall be saved; but he that believeth not shall be damned. And these signs shall follow them that believe; In my name shall they cast out devils; they shall speak with new tongues; They shall take up serpents; and if they drink any deadly thing, it shall not hurt them; they shall lay hands on the sick, and they shall recover. So then after the Lord had spoken unto them, he was received up into heaven, and sat on the right hand of God. And they went forth, and preached every where, the Lord working with them, and confirming the word with signs following. Amen.

—Mark 16:15-20

The Spirit of the Lord is upon me, because he hath anointed me to preach the gospel to the poor; he hath sent me to heal the brokenhearted, to preach deliverance to the captives, and recovering of sight to the blind, to set at liberty them that are bruised, To preach the acceptable year of the Lord.

—Luke 4:18,19

He that believeth on me, as the scripture hath said, out of his belly shall flow rivers of living water.

—John 7:38

Verily, verily, I say unto you, He that believeth on me, the works that I do shall he do also; and greater works than these shall he do; because I go unto my Father. And whatsoever ye shall ask in my name, that will I do, that the Father may be glorified in the Son.

—John 14:12,13

And believers were the more added to the Lord, multitudes both of men and women. Insomuch that they brought forth the sick into the streets, and laid them on beds and couches, that at the least the shadow of Peter passing by might overshadow some of them.

—Acts 5:14,15

How God anointed Jesus of Nazareth with the Holy Ghost and with power: who went about doing good, and healing all that were oppressed of the devil; for God was with him.

—Acts 10:38

And God wrought special miracles by the hands of Paul: So that from his body were brought unto the sick handkerchiefs or aprons, and the diseases departed from them, and the evil spirits went out of them.

—Acts 19:11,12

So then faith cometh by hearing, and hearing by the word of God.

—Romans 10:17

For the kingdom of God is not in word, but in power.

—1 Corinthians 4:20

But we have this treasure in earthen vessels, that the excellency of the power may be of God, and not of us.

—2 Corinthians 4:7

Now unto him that is able to do exceeding abundantly above all that we ask or think, according to the power that worketh in us.

—Ephesians 3:20

But unto the Son he saith, Thy throne, O God, is for ever and ever: a sceptre of righteousness is the sceptre of thy kingdom. Thou hast loved righteousness, and hated iniquity; therefore God, even thy God, hath anointed thee with the oil of gladness above thy fellows.

—Hebrews 1:8,9

Is any sick among you? let him call for the elders of the church; and let them pray over him, anointing him with oil in the name of the Lord: And the prayer of faith shall save the sick, and the Lord shall raise him up; and if he have committed sins, they shall be forgiven him.

—James 5:14,15

But ye have an unction from the Holy One, and ye know all things.

—1 John 2:20

But the anointing which ye have received of him abideth in you, and ye need not that any man teach you: but as the same anointing teacheth you of all things, and is truth, and is no lie, and even as it hath taught you, ye shall abide in him.

—1 John 2:27

Beloved, now are we the sons of God, and it doth not yet appear what we shall be: but we know that, when he shall appear, we shall be like him; for we shall see him as he is.

—1 John 3:2

He that committeth sin is of the devil; for the devil sinneth from the beginning. For this purpose the Son of God was manifested, that he might destroy the works of the devil.

—1 John 3:8

And they overcame him by the blood of the Lamb, and by the word of their testimony; and they loved not their lives unto the death.

—Revelation 12:11

ABOUT THE AUTHOR

ROD PARSLEY, bestselling author of more than sixty books, is the dynamic pastor of World Harvest Church in Columbus, Ohio, a church with worldwide ministries and a global outreach. As a highly sought-after crusade and conference speaker whom God has raised up as a prophetic voice to America and the world, Parsley is calling people to Jesus Christ through the good news of the Gospel.

He oversees Bridge of Hope Missions, Harvest Preparatory School, World Harvest Bible College, and the *Breakthrough* broadcast, a Christian television and radio show seen by millions and broadcast to nearly 200 countries around the world, including a potential viewing audience of 97% of the homes in the United States and 78% in Canada. *Breakthrough* is carried on 1,400 stations and cable affiliates, including the Trinity Broadcasting Network, the Canadian Vision Network, Armed Forces Radio and Television Network, and in several countries spanning the globe.

Parsley's refreshingly direct style encourages Christians to examine and eradicate sin from their lives. A fearless champion of living God's way, Parsley follows the high standard set by Jesus Christ and compels his readers to do the same. He and his wife Joni have two children, Ashton and Austin.

OTHER BOOKS BY ROD PARSLEY

Ancient Wells, Living Water

At the Cross, Where Healing Begins

Could It Be?

Daily Breakthroughs

Don't Look Now

The Day Before Eternity

He Came First

It's Already There – Where Are You?

No Dry Season (Bestseller)

No More Crumbs (Bestseller)

On the Brink (#1 Bestseller)

Preparing for the Glory

Repairers of the Breach

Silent No More

Tribulation to Triumph

What To Do When It's Just Not Working . . .

Look Again!

For more information about *Breakthrough*,
World Harvest Church, Center for Moral Clarity,
World Harvest Bible College, Harvest Preparatory School,
or to receive a product list of the many books, CD's and
DVD's by Rod Parsley, write or call:

Breakthrough/World Harvest Church
P.O. Box 32932
Columbus, OH 43232-0932 USA
(614) 837-1990 (Office)
www.breakthrough.net

World Harvest Bible College
P.O. Box 32901
Columbus, OH 43232-0901 USA
(614) 837-4088
www.worldharvestbiblecollege.org

Harvest Preparatory School
P.O. Box 32903
Columbus, OH 43232-0903 USA
(614) 837-1990
www.harvestprep.org

Center for Moral Clarity
P.O. Box 32903
Columbus, OH 43232-9926 USA
(613) 382-1188
www.CenterForMoralClarity.net

If you need prayer, Breakthrough Prayer Warriors are
ready to pray with you 24 hours a day, 7 days a week
at: (888) 534-3838